It's None of *Your* *Business*

A Complete Guide to Protecting Your Privacy, Identity & Assets

By Larry: Sontag

It's None of Your Business
A Complete Guide to Protecting Your Privacy, Identity & Assets

by Larry: Sontag

Disclaimer: The author of this book is not a legal or financial advisor and recommends that you pursue sufficient means to assure yourself of the legality of all privacy and financial strategies. Nothing contained herein may be construed to be legal advice. Please verify all information upon which you may rely. The contents of this publication are for information and research only.

Third Edition May 2000

ISBN 0-9674354-0-4

Published in the United States
by PMI Enterprises, Woodinville, Washington

Printed in the United States by
Morris Publishing • 3212 East Highway 30 • Kearney, NE 68847
1-800-650-7888

A monthly newsletter is available from PMI to keep you informed about the latest tricks and schemes of business and governments to invade your privacy. It also includes strategies and analysis of news and legislation to help you protect yourself. Books and other privacy related products are available in quantity from PMI at discounted prices. For information on prices, terms and ordering contact PMI Enterprises toll free at (877) 234-2854 or visit the PMI web site at www.privacysupport.com. PMI Enterprises operates with all reservation of rights and is not a tax withholding agent.

Table of Contents

Introduction

From an *Associated Press* story, July 8, 1998: Thirteen years ago, a Florida man assumed a new identity from a driver's license stolen from a recreational vehicle dealer in central Oregon. As time went on, the victim, from Medford, Oregon, lost his perfect credit rating, his right to vote, and nearly landed in jail. He was threatened with arrest for jumping bail!

The story goes on to detail how Mr. Stan Smith (not his real name), who took years to build up a perfect credit rating, and could borrow $100,000 on his name, couldn't even get a department store credit card. He had to get a new driver's license and Social Security Number and couldn't even vote because the criminal who stole his identity had changed his registration address. It all started with a stolen wallet. He nearly got arrested for outstanding warrants and has been living a financial nightmare for years. The criminal, who stole his wallet and admitted buying a $23,000 Dodge pickup under Smith's name, got only six months in jail for first degree aggravated theft. Unfortunately Mr. Smith's nightmare will go on for years to come.

Another story from the *Associated Press*, July 20, 1998 details how a man from Mesa, Arizona lost his wallet back in 1947. It was recovered and he thought the matter had ended. Well, not only had it not ended, it had just begun! The person who found the wallet was apprehended in Portland 51 years later on an outstanding federal warrant for false statements and criminal acts involving suspected Medicare fraud. The victim, who we will call Ralph, was on the same railroad track crew as the alleged thief, David Gonzales. Soon after the loss, Ralph's high school principal in Benson, Arizona received a phone call from the police in Albuquerque, New Mexico saying that they had him in jail. The principal told police that it was impossible, because Ralph was in class! He got his ID papers back and thought the matter was resolved, but late in 1997, he received a letter from Oregon food stamp officials saying that he had been overpaid by $285 worth of food stamps. Ralph, who was then a retired supervisor of Mesa's refuse collection program had never *lived* in Oregon and had never used food stamps! Apparently Mr. Gonzales had kept the ID numbers for over 50 years!

Then Ralph got a letter from the IRS. They claimed that there was some discrepancy between his records and they thought he lived in Portland, Oregon. Furthermore, Oregon Health Sciences University started sending statements to him at his home in Mesa, Arizona, asking him to sign various forms. Soon after that, he was refused insurance coverage on a prescription refill at his local pharmacy because they said he didn't have insurance anymore. His health maintenance organization, which provided his Medicare coverage, said that some guy had called and wanted to cancel his coverage because he'd moved to Portland. It took an attorney five weeks to get his insurance reinstated.

The problem continued when Ralph tried to refinance his house. The mortgage company said they couldn't because he was behind on some payments to some doctors. He had $6500 in outstanding Medicare coinsurance bills for medical treatment delivered in Oregon. Apparently Gonzales had built up over $32,000 in medical bills during 1997 and 1998, much of which had been paid by Medicare in Oregon. While all of this was going on Ralph had been telling people that his ID was stolen and being used by someone else, but no one believed him! Even though a person has finally been arrested, you can bet that this story isn't over yet.

Finally, imagine you are a fourteen year old girl with an opportunity for a photo shoot with a local modeling agency. You are asked to change into leotards for a few pictures, which could land you a big contract for modeling or acting! The picture taking is conducted very normally and without incident, but the next day you find out that the photographer has been arrested for child pornography. All the kids at school are calling you the porno-queen! Where did he get any pornographic pictures of you? Well, you saw the camera he held during the shoot, but you did *not* see the one in the dressing room! Sure the guy got arrested, but how do you salvage your *life*?

The above stories illustrate the importance of your physical and financial identity. The rapid dissemination of information about your official identity, especially via computer records, has dramatically increased the chances of your life being turned completely upside down with the loss of any personal identification documents. A hundred years ago, a lost wallet would be an inconvenience, today it could be devastating. Along with your identifying papers and official documents, you give the finder or the thief the ability to literally become you in the eyes of the credit, medical, and legal world. Identity and credit theft is one of the fastest growing crimes in America today resulting in over $1 billion in losses annually.

With the proliferation of computer systems, the Internet, and the integration of medical, social, official, and financial records, we have all become slaves to a system that increasingly controls our every act. Legislation establishing a national ID will make this an even greater threat, allowing government or corporate bureaucrats and common thieves to literally dictate our very livelihoods should they get control of our official number.

Technology isn't always our friend. Hidden recording devices can catch crooks, but can also catch innocent people in the act of performing perfectly normal everyday activities. While you may not be breaking any laws, you don't want everyone on the planet to be watching everything you do. What is rapidly happening in our world is that governments are increasingly using crime control as an excuse to monitor our every act. Businesses, especially the information industry, is analyzing and recording our purchasing habits, while the government records everything else about us. Together, our freedoms are being eroded at an alarming pace, as choices become more determined for us, and we are forced into asking permission to conduct everyday activities. As you will see, the forces of complete control are hard at work and our ability to determine our own lives is becoming more and more difficult ... but it can be done.

Personal privacy has nearly been abolished, but secrecy in government and big business has been elevated to the status of most holy, sovereign, sanctified, and canonized rule of law among all the nations of the world. Everyone else seems to have access to information cataloguing all the most intimate and important details of your personal, medical, financial, spiritual and political life, but you do not.

If you believe that there really is no conspiracy, that you can still do what you want to do, and your life really isn't being controlled, read on. There are representatives in Congress and the White House, in the parliaments of Canada and the European nations, and in the UN right now who really do have a plan for you. In the name of controlling illegal immigration, eliminating welfare fraud, and getting deadbeat parents to support their children, politicians are conspiring to destroy the last vestiges of privacy we currently have. National medical ID's, coupled with standardized licenses of all types containing everyone's Social Security or Social Insurance Number are only the tip of the iceberg. Centralized governmental files, containing all pertinent citizen records from birth certificates to library card charges are in the planning stages. These would be indexed and searched via retinal scans and DNA samples. Are you going down to the store for a carton of milk? Better have your national ID card! Need your teeth cleaned? Don't forget your ID. Want to walk down the street or take a plane and visit grandma? Not without your ID! Need a job? Forget it without your official ID. If nothing is done to stop it, you will soon have to produce a federally approved identification card for just about everything you now take for granted. Just what country do we live in? Are we really free?

Can this truly be happening? Has everyone forgotten why people came to America? There's not even a national outcry against this outrageous attack on our Constitutional rights. Congress, led by a few prominent Republicans, is moving rapidly and almost without opposition toward complete control of your everyday life! President Clinton leads the Democratic side in this scheme, especially through his proposed national health care program. The national medical ID requirement was from a line buried in the Health Insurance Portability and Accountability Act of 1996, requiring Health and Human Services to create a standard identifying number for anyone requesting health care. It passed 98-0 in the Senate and 421-2 in the House! Does anyone *read* those bills, or are our representatives really in *favor* of this? Fortunately, after much criticism, mainly from privacy rights groups, the administration has agreed to postpone the medical ID requirement until a better method of protecting privacy is developed. President Clinton, in spite of his public proclamations of support for privacy has done more to destroy your privacy rights and safety than any other president in the history of the United States. He, along with former President George Bush, and others before him, have led us on a road to complete identification and control. You are being branded, my friend. There's not much difference between an internal passport/national ID card and a number written on your wrist. Wasn't there a country in central Europe that did this back in the 30's and 40's?

Perhaps we take our rights for granted. How easily they can disappear! Speaking of rights, just what *are* our rights? Let me ask you something. Do you have a right to buy something from someone without *anyone* else knowing about it? Do you have the right to trade one item of value for another item of value with whomever you wish and without reporting it to another human being anywhere on this earth? Do you have a right to work for another person and agree to exchange your labor for something of value without *anyone* else knowing about it? Do you have the right to live anywhere you want in America? Do you even have a right to move to a new town without reporting your move to anyone else? Do you have the right to go down to your doctor and get treatment for a medical condition, expecting that what you confide to him or her will not leave the office?

Maybe its about time that we started *thinking* about our rights. Most of us studied the Constitution in high school, but would have a difficult time finding a copy of it anywhere in our homes. And most people only have a vague recollection of what's in it. Is there anywhere in the Constitution a clause that guarantees us the right to privacy? Well, no, not specifically. The 4th Amendment states: The right of the people to be secure in their persons, houses, papers, and effects, against unreasonable searches and seizures, shall not be violated. Does this mean that someone cannot snoop on you? Does this mean that businesses you patronize can't reveal every detail of your financial dealings with them without your permission? Does this protect you from overzealous bureaucrats on fishing expeditions? If you think you are protected by law against invasions of your privacy, you are indeed misguided. Most of the laws on the books that have the word privacy in them actually do more to destroy your privacy than to protect it. You're going to have to take care of yourself, and that is where this book comes in. I'm going to show you *who* is snooping on you, *how* they do it, *what* they find out, and *what you can do to stop it*! Fortunately there is a lot that you can do, and it's not usually expensive or complicated.

Nancy Reagan said it most succinctly: Just say no! If you don't remember anything else about this book, remember this: you don't have to tell everyone who asks, everything about yourself, just because they ask! You don't have to fill out every space on a form just because it's there! You don't have to reveal your Social Security Number, driver's license number, credit card number, address, phone, date of birth, mother's maiden name, and the city where you were born, just because someone asks! JUST SAY NO! There, I said it, now get on with your life.

The trouble is, you already blew it, or your parents did. Even newborns are routinely given Social Security or Social Insurance Numbers, hardly before they take their first breath!

The U.S. government has an official program designed to trick people into thinking that their children have to have a Social Security Number before they leave the hospital. Remember that the Social Security Number is still *completely voluntary* in the U.S. as is the Social Insurance Number in Canada. Branding you with an identification number is the first step in taking away your privacy. You, your movements, and your transactions, can now be traced. Welcome to earth.

Let's say that you have made it all the way through high school and have lived a very boring, conventional life. You haven't had your first job yet. You haven't registered for the selective service. All you've done is go to public school. Sorry, you're probably already in a hundred different databases. Whoa you say, what databases am I in and do I really want to be there? Does it matter? Why should I care? I haven't done anything wrong, except maybe to tease my little sister a few times when I was younger. You, my friend, have only just begun. You're about to leave the life of a child, under the control and care of your parents, to begin a life under the control (but not always the care) of government and businesses entities who see you more as a source of income than as anything else. Now that I think of it, people have been telling me for years that I was a cynic, but I never really thought of myself as one. Perhaps I am a cynic, but I am now one with a mission, that is to help you be free. We are lucky, because all is not lost. You may have lost your privacy and become a mere number in vast databases which catalog your every move, but you *can opt out*. You can just say no. You can conduct your personal and financial life with true anonymity. I will show you how after I have shown you what you're up against.

Why do people lock their doors, guard their children, check out contractors who will paint their homes, and spend hours researching a stock to invest in, yet they give out all forms of personal, medical, and financial information daily to strangers who may or may not have their best interests at heart and who may even be convicted felons? Perhaps they don't know how easy it is for criminals to use personal information against them to steal their money, property, and even their very identity.

In this book, you will find out how easy it is for *anyone* to find out all the intimate details of your personal, medical, educational, social, and financial life. You will learn how criminals, marketers, and government agencies regularly share and use your personal information for purposes that are detrimental to your well being and to that of your family. I am not trying to make us all completely paranoid, but my purpose is to open your eyes to what is going on so that you may gain the means with which to protect yourself. Americans especially, think that they live in the land of the free, yet they little realize how controlled they are and how much *more* controlled they are to *become*. I will attempt to expose the degree to which government bureaucrats are even now planning to brand every citizen with identifying marks or required papers so that their every activity can be monitored and controlled. I will attempt to show you how your desire for convenience and your avoidance of controversy puts you at risk every day. The government and corporate entities have grown so large, that little is available to protect individual rights. Bureaucrats and corporate officials are able to control who, what, where, when and how common purchases are made by everyone in the world. They control the citizenry by controlling the money supply, which means they want to know about every transaction you make. A discussion about money and the international banking system is at the following web site: www.parascope.com/mx/fedm.htm.

This is by no means the sole purpose of this book. Every day innocent people are tracked down by their Social Security Number and threatened by others who have a grudge against them or to whom they owe money. I am also writing because everyone deserves to be able to live a life free from fear, free from the threat of someone being able to track them down and ruin their lives. Whenever citizens are required to have an all-encompassing identifying number, there is a chance that another person can find that number and cause them harm, or equally as bad, that a computer data error will cause enormous damage to their reputation, credit, or chances for a job. After nearly 20 years in the computer industry as a database programmer, I have yet to find one client who can keep clean records. Databases are riddled with errors.

When it comes to standardization, you will find there's usually little or none. For example, Bill Johnson's full name might be William James Johnson, Jr. III, yet it might be entered into a record as:

Bill Johnson
William Johnson
William J. Johnson
Bill J Johnson
Bill J. Johnson
Bill Johnson III

If you think that all of the information that everyone is keeping on you is complete and correct, especially if you have ever moved, married, divorced, had children, changed phone numbers, or changed jobs, think again. The files containing this ever-changing information also must track millions of people who may have the same names, and the data includes those who have been born and died over the past century. After checking through thousands of clients' records to find errors, or make sure they were entering data correctly, I can assure you, *your* records are both incorrect *and* incomplete. This doesn't mean that your bank has mistakes in your checking account or that the police really think you are a criminal, but it *does* mean that in all of the thousands of databases you're in, there are mistakes. I'm not saying that there *may* be mistakes, I'm saying that there *are* mistakes! The trouble is, you don't even know what files you're in, let alone, what information is kept there or how to correct or remove it.

This book is not just about privacy and keeping your PIN number secret. It's about your right of free travel, your right to contract, your right to accept or not accept benefits from the government, and your right to privacy in your medical records.

It's about your right to freely conduct business with another human being as long as that transaction does not impinge on the rights of others. It's about your right to work for a living and contract with an employer for your services in exchange for anything of value, including money. Privacy in the context of *freedom* includes being able to interact with other people without someone recording your every act! It means that you can go about your business without worrying that you're breaking some obscure, paranoia inspired law. It means that you can freely travel about the country and indeed the world, without wondering if your every move is being traced and possibly used to concoct some criminal scenario. If you are concerned about your freedoms and constitutional rights, you are not alone. There are many organizations who are working actively to protect these rights, but you need to get involved and that starts with educating yourself. Just keep in mind that the more you standardize yourself and become a number, the easier it is for that number to be used against you.

The great thing about writing this book, is that I can tell you how you can *regain* your privacy and your freedom. All is not lost. There are people out there who are concerned about your constitutional rights and have developed ways for you to exert them, without landing you in jail. You *can* get your privacy and your anonymity back, so that you can conduct your affairs as you see fit, without some government or corporate bureaucrat making the decision for you, as if you were a child. My belief is that you as an adult, have as great an ability to decide what to do with your life as anyone else. If you don't think you've given away your independence and relinquished control of your finances to large corporations, just try cutting up all your credit cards. Try quitting your job and doing something you'd *really* like to do for a living, instead of the daily commute and eight hour day! You'll find out that your friendly bank is all of a sudden not so friendly, and the creditors who were only too willing to extend more credit may now be your worst enemies. There *are* remedies though. You can be free, and you can make your own decisions. Remember, knowledge is power. I recommend that you continue your education with the resources listed at the end of this book, and take advantage of the many ways to regain your privacy and your rights. The journey may seem unfamiliar, but the rewards are well worth it. Don't forget that you have been educated to think that our current system is the best in the world, but you need to open your mind to new facts so that you can come to know what you are dealing with in your quest to be free and so that you will understand how an elite few operate to control you.

This book is written for the average citizen. It makes frequent reference to the U.S. government and American entities, but is applicable to all of the modern world, as corporations and governments have become so interconnected, that sometimes it is difficult to tell where one stops and the other starts. It is written for everyone who desires to be free and wants to make their own decisions in life. You don't have to be rich or have a great deal of possessions to benefit from this book, you just have to want to be a natural human inhabitant of the planet, with the desire to interact with your fellow inhabitants as you see fit. I guarantee, there are many out there who would like you to remain a slave to the system. You can exert your rights, but you must know the rules of the game, so that you won't be inadvertently tripped up doing something that is totally harmless and benevolent, but which threatens the power and control of those who supposedly have sworn to serve you.

The section on strategies includes information for those wishing to remain in the system and lead relatively conventional lives, and for those who wish to be more independent (including completely sovereign). You can choose the level of privacy and freedom you want for yourself and your family. There will be challenges, but the returns are great. Let freedom live.

I. Who's Spying on You and How?

Video, audio, and electronic surveillance

Video surveillance seems to be in every store, every lobby, every elevator, every public building, even on many street corners and it's spreading daily. It's in public squares, on the highway, at work, even in people's houses as they watch their baby sitters and nannies. There are even companies that sell mock video surveillance cameras for those who can't afford the real thing. They have been found just about everywhere, sometimes installed by a company or public institution for security purposes, sometimes by voyeuristic employees, and sometimes by others who gain access to the building for the purpose of expanding their collection of video tapes. Nowhere is safe: public bathrooms, gyms, schools (public and private), modeling agencies, suntan salons, YMCA's and YWCA's, clothing stores' dressing rooms, hotels and motels, public and private swimming pools, rented houses and apartments, just about anywhere you find people changing their clothes, you have the chance of finding a hidden camera. There are cases of people renting apartments which contain several cameras, hidden in smoke detectors, electrical or cable TV outlets, lights, behind ventilation grates, and in holes drilled in the ceiling. You name it, a camera has probably been hidden there. The components have become small enough to fit in the eye of a teddy bear or in the frames of eyeglasses. Some people have even purchased special video cameras that hook up to their computers and allow them to go on display at home 24 hours a day over the Internet. Whether these people just like the attention, or for whatever other reason, they are exposing more than their lifestyles to the general public. It would be entirely possible to determine the location and wait for a time to burglarize the house (or rape the occupant). The U.S. government is even using a scanner in major airports that can see through clothing (all in the name of controlling guns and drugs).

What most people don't know, is that most of the above surveillance isn't even illegal. Most states have no laws against video surveillance, and may only have laws that make it illegal to audio tape someone without their permission. These same states probably require both persons to know about any taping that is done over the telephone, but the federal law requires only that one person give permission. Now if you don't mind someone watching you in the bathroom and shower, just as long as they don't tape anything you *say*, well, then I suppose there's no problem. Do you mind if voyeurs take pictures of you and/or your children and then put them on the Internet or sell the tapes to the public? Perhaps you don't have anything to hide, but do you know what is done with all the information (and video or audio tapes) that others are gathering on you? Is it accurate? What is it used for? Could it be borrowed or sold to others who might be able to use your identity (and your nice clean record and credit) or your pictures for pornographic purposes?

In the late 1700's, the British political philosopher Jeremy Bentham came up with a plan for a modern prison called the panopticon, from the Greek word panoptes, meaning all-seeing. At the center of this circular prison would be a tower with windows where guards could see into every prisoner's cell. It was to be a system of total surveillance. Bentham, who saw it as a benevolent penal colony, said, "To be incessantly under the eyes of the inspector is to lose in effect the power to do evil and almost the thought of wanting to do it." The philosopher Michel Foucault agreed that in a system of total surveillance, there is no need for arms, physical violence, or material constraints, just a gaze. But he also saw a sinister aspect. In the end, Foucault said in the 1970's, each individual will internalize this gaze to the point that he is his own supervisor ... exercising this surveillance over and against himself. If we were all actually under surveillance at all times, or just *thought* we were, it would make real surveillance unnecessary. George Orwell's world of 1984 would be a reality. You would never be sure if the TV you were watching was watching you back. The government agents who's job it was to watch over us, could target anyone, anytime. Since you never know, you have to assume it was always on. If you haven't read Orwell's *1984* you must, but finish this book first. There's a lot at stake.

Today there is so much surveillance that we have already become used to it. One of the biggest problems is that we're so trusting and don't complain about it. A lot of people even support *more* surveillance, in the name of crime control. How quickly we forget history, thinking it can't happen here. What is our assurance that our freedoms are secure? Well, we have our political system, we can vote, and we have the Constitution. And so we let it happen, because no one is shooting at us from afar and there is relative peace in the streets. Like the Germans replied after World War II, when asked how they could let Hitler take control, they said, "We all had jobs and the trains ran on time." We are like the frog who would jump out of boiling water, but dies when put in warm water which is slowly heated. Today guns are not needed to take control of a country. The only thing that is really important is control of the money supply. If people think that someone is watching them, and every financial transaction is recorded for possible scrutiny, they will submit to whatever rules are imposed for them. It doesn't matter which political party is in office. What does matter is who controls the security agencies, the bureaucracies, the corporate monopolies, and the international banks. Are you willing to let others observe and record everything you do and then pass judgment on it to determine if it is *permitted* according to *their* idea of morality, or economic well-being? The best interests of a large corporation do not necessarily coincide with yours! If you're counting on the law to protect you from plain voyeurs, overzealous corporate intelligence departments, or government agencies looking for something to do, you are going to be sorely disappointed!

Government agencies

The U.S. government maintains databases on virtually everyone in the country. It must truly be one of the most paranoid governments on earth, as it operates the largest and most invasive spy network anywhere. Some have suggested that, with the end of the Cold War, spy agencies need to justify their existence (read jobs and big budgets here), so they are now doing so by spying on everyone, not just the supposed *enemy*. Of course there are always terrorists to investigate, and *everyone* is a potential terrorist! One method of controlling terrorists is to control their access to money. If their assets can be tracked down and frozen, they are less able to buy weapons. Another task the spy agencies have taken on is corporate espionage. They routinely listen in on *all* phone conversations and then pass on important information to selected corporations.

One primary source of this information is the IRS (Revenue Canada in that country). Every year, you voluntarily provide the government with vital information about your finances, travel, personal habits, and employment. In a *New York Times* article dated April 9, 1997, The IRS admitted that it has not reduced the improper browsing of taxpayer records by its agents. 1,515 such cases have become known in the two years prior to the report. A study of the EARL (Electronic Audit Research Log) software program indicates that, some employees, when encountered, indicated they browsed because they do not believe it is wrong and that there will be little consequence to them if they are caught. About 51,000 IRS employees have access to taxpayer records through the Integrated Data Retrieval System. Recent court rulings have decided that these invasions of privacy are not illegal as long as the information is not given to others (of course that is impossible to determine). The Senate is debating legislation to levy heavy fines and imprisonment for violators, but none currently exists. The GAO has also determined, according to their recent report on these abuses, that 6,400 tapes and cartridges which might contain taxpayer information are also *missing*.

The IRS is an excellent snooper, but not a very good record keeper. Their mainframe equipment is old, subject to breakdown, and not well integrated between offices. They have over 88,000 computer programs on over 80 mainframe computers, containing more than 80 million lines of code. In 1997, a multi-billion dollar fully integrated computer system that was supposed to modernize the agency was completely discarded because it didn't work. Offices often can hardly communicate with each other and the current system is so decrepit that breakdowns are a daily occurrence. Government studies also find that the IRS is one of the agencies least ready for the year 2000. By the end of 1997, they had only cleaned up 2,000 of their 88,000 programs! Still, the IRS maintains what are called Individual Master Files on every taxpayer in the country. A legal researcher who has been decoding these files for the past eight years has reported that he has only found *one* clean file, ie. one with no errors. The rest had wrong codes in them indicating that the person was perhaps a suspected drug dealer, tax protester, or money launderer. The IRS can easily get a search warrant against someone who has erroneous codes in their file and the U.S. Supreme Court has ruled that the responsibility for the accuracy of these files lies with the individual citizen. Most people don't even know that these files exist, much less what the cryptic codes mean! If you ever get audited or face liens, levies, or seizures, you might want to take a serious look at your file! You might be surprised at what you've been up to. See organizations in the resources section for how to get in touch with someone to help you see what's in your files and how to decode the codes.

If an accounting firm was discovered to be handling one in four clients illegally, what do you think would happen? If an internal audit revealed that FedEx sent one in four packages to a wrong destination, would anyone use them anymore? Or what if you found out that one out of four hamburgers that McDonald's sold had health threatening levels of e-coli bacteria, would you ever go there again? What would happen to these large, well established companies? After some severe losses, there would be some definite changes in management, and everyone in the country would know about it! Some might even be sent to jail! Yet, two internal audits from the IRS have revealed that one in four property seizures by that agency were handled improperly and in many cases illegally. The audits are in response to a series of hearings held by Senate Finance Committee Chairman Bill Roth of Delaware who called the results of the audits a stunning confession of the sins of the IRS.

Unfortunately, the IRS is not governed by the same rules as business. Even with the 1998 reform bill that passed both houses of Congress with a total of eight dissenting votes, the real problem remains. The IRS is powerful precisely because nearly every taxpayer fears the agency and the ever expanding federal bureaucracy wants your money. Don't believe that the IRS is any more warm and friendly than it ever was!

Lets take a look at some of the IRS's friendly ways, as revealed by the audits. The IRS tried to force a severely ill man to sell the home occupied by his wife and two daughters and only backed off because the man died and the agent felt the sale would engender bad publicity. The IRS didn't pursue alternatives to property seizure, disregarded mandatory waiting periods proscribed by law and in some cases didn't even contact taxpayers before seizing their property. This is patently illegal and even against internal IRS regulations! Some people are even now pursuing suits against IRS agents who aren't following the rules. The auditors said that IRS agents sometimes seized property of little value and demonstrated a lack of adequate concern for the taxpayer's medical and financial needs. In one case, the IRS seized and subsequently sold a vehicle owned by an unemployed woman whose husband was terminally ill. The woman had had knee surgery and couldn't work; she was facing another operation and her terminally ill husband had to live with his mother in another city. The IRS got a total of $6,100 for the automobile and artwork it contained. Finally, there is a case of the IRS seizing both vehicles from a family who had two, but who had asked that they be left with one so that they could get a son to the hospital when he had seizures (which happened frequently, some of which required hospitalization). The IRS said callously that the medical concerns of the family were not their affair and both cars would be seized. So much for a kindler, gentler IRS! Really makes you want to tell them everything about your finances each April 15th doesn't it?

The government also tracks personal information about people through registrations such as gun ownership, business and professional licenses, student loans, school enrollment, library cards, voter registration, and even dog licenses. The federal government is currently pressuring states to *require* a Social Security Number to purchase such things as fishing, hunting, and driver's licenses. The feds want Social Security Numbers on all licenses by October 1, 2000 and is threatening to withhold federal block grants if they don't get their way, so any legislator who opposes them is accused of denying children of their state the needed funds for all the programs that affect them! Ostensibly this is to help track down deadbeat parents and control illegal immigration. So we all lose our privacy because of the irresponsibility of a few! Fingerprints, digitized photos, and Social Security Numbers *are* required in many states already. Recently it was revealed that the Secret Service was behind a company in New Hampshire purchasing millions of driver's license photos ostensibly to run an anti-fraud campaign in Colorado, South Carolina, and Florida. Officials in these states are now trying to get the photos back and/or cancel the contracts, but the company says that it's all legal and their system is of great value, so they're not about to return anything. No one was told that a million and a half Secret Service dollars supported the effort which turned ordinary citizens license photos into mug shots, to be sold to anyone willing to pay.

National identifiers are also sneaking into the health care system. Social Security Number's have been used for a long time to identify and record patients, even though by law, you are not even required to have one. But now, if you are a health care provider, the federal government is proposing rules for implementation of the National Provider Identification (NPI) Registry which will allow them to track the whereabouts and practice of every health care provider in the country, and may allow access to the medical records of patients. All health care professionals, whether or not they participate in federal or state health care programs, must apply to Enumerators which will provide them with a new federal identification number. Penalties for noncompliance may be severe. The NPI Registry was part of administrative simplification which was enacted in the 1996 Health Insurance Portability and Accountability Act (HIPAA). The Clinton administration is pushing hard for a national health ID number, which of course would be your Social Security Number.

What does all of this registration and national identification mean? Well it means that the government can track and control your every movement. It can provide *or deny* you access to the most basic services, like driving and health care. Actually, your life can be controlled by a *computer* somewhere. Do you belong to a political or religious group that the present administration doesn't like? Sorry, your national ID card doesn't seem to be working ma'am. Are you engaged in a controversial profession that some FBI agent or NSA bureaucrat doesn't approve of? Sorry sir, your purchase of groceries is not approved according to information supplied by your national ID card. Did you ever vote for a candidate disliked by the current administration? We're sorry sir, your electric service will be terminated in 24 hours because of lack of payment (even though you have always paid on time). Think it can't happen here, in the land of the free? Think again. The Clinton administration has been accused of asking for IRS audits on scores of critics and illegally using the FBI to harass its enemies. Even if the government *always* had your best interests in mind and *always* followed the tenets of the Constitution, computer glitches and incorrect data finds it way into files every day. Then there are the thousands of clerks who enter all the data into those files or have access to them and could change anything anytime. Don't think you're immune from this happening to you just because it's never happened before.

Other governments aren't any more secure in the data they compile on citizens. A story out of Quebec tells of government employees treating confidential information casually and sometimes even taking sneak peeks at files, says the province's access-to-information commissioner. In some cases, it's the result of a lack of concern, in other cases it's also a lack of knowledge and sometimes a certain casualness with regard to the law, commissioner Paul-Andre Comeau told a news conference. The province's Access to Information Commission looked into the problem after nine government employees were fired in the fall of 1997 for abusing confidential information or selling it, mainly to detective agencies. There are cases of voyeurism, there are cases of disrespect, Comeau said. Who's business is it anyway, if an individual takes Prozac or whether a young girl has had an abortion? Do you care if your personal history, your psychological, medical, employment, financial, educational, professional, recreational, and lifestyle records are sold to anyone willing to pay?

CSE (Communications Security Establishment), Canada's super-secret spy agency is not legally able to spy on its own citizens just as the NSA is restricted in the United States, but these agencies work together, with one agency spying on the citizens of the other country and then sharing the information. Large government agencies around the world are working under extremely strict security, revealing what they do to only a very select group of individuals, some of which may not be even elected representatives. As a matter of fact, it is very difficult for those in Congress to find out what is going on in these agencies even though they fund the programs. Even the *budgets* of these agencies are hidden from most members of Congress. Government employees from the local cop on the beat to the head of the FBI or NSA are increasingly acting more like the master and less like the public servants they are supposed to be, all in the name of fighting crime. Recently a congressional oversight committee asked for a report on the practices of the National Security Agency and was *refused*!. The director of the NSA sited *attorney/client privilege!* Government agencies around the world have literally gotten completely out of control and many are totally unaccountable to their constituents.

The *New York Post* reports June 28,1998, that police have been ordered to write down the license plates of cars parked near troublesome bars and nightclubs even *before* a crime is committed. The directive was designed to give detectives a leg up on finding witnesses or suspects if a crime occurred and was issued by former Chief of Patrol Wilbur Chapman, who was selected by Mayor Giuliani to be the city's new Department of Transportation commissioner. In like manner, some states require all felons to give up DNA samples to make it easier to investigate them in the future. Legislation has also been suggested that ALL citizens give up DNA samples so that police could merely gather evidence at the scene and compare it with samples from the entire country. If you happened to touch something at the scene of a crime, even innocently, you would be a subject. What further new ideas do you think will be in store for New Yorkers going about their lives, whether publicly or privately? How about control and tracking of subway riders?

New York City is on its way to scrapping the MetroCard# in favor of issuing smartcards (transponders) for riders. Reason: so cards can be read without current swiping problems. The card would be detected in your pocket. Reportedly, this kind of tracking is already in effect in Singapore. What do smartcard transit cards mean? If a crime occurs somewhere, the police will be able to call in for questioning all people in the area who used transit at the time. And, of course, full tracking of your movements, from bus/subway to toll bridges (EZ-PASS transponders) would be a private investigator's dream. In New York City, the FBI spent millions of dollars to install a permanent fully-functional real-time physical tracking network. Needless to say, the FBI did not make a public announcement. It consists of a citywide network of hidden sensing devices that pick up signals from a moving vehicle and immediately projects the precise location on a large illuminated map located in the FBI's Manhattan command post. The FBI denied a request for a tour. In 1993, however, it allowed a visit by a reporter who was working on what the bureau expected would be a friendly article. The command center, she later wrote, looks similar to the Starship Enterprise, of *Star Trek*. On the rear wall of the room are three giant screens projecting neighborhood maps, live field surveillance, and graphs, charting the progress of a manhunt. Law enforcement officials can watch and direct as criminals are caught in the act. Their computer mouse screen pointers are a gun icon.

It is also reported that the recent renovation of Madison Square Garden included the installation of hundreds of cameras, all connected to large databases containing photos of suspected terrorists. If a face matches, security agents are ready to spring out instantly and apprehend or "eliminate" the threat.

No matter where you live in the country, you are tracked, by post office change of address forms, marriage licenses, deeds, driver's licenses, mortgages, liens, Assessor's records, court records including any arrests or tickets, registration and fingerprinting for selective service or public school teaching, birth certificates, adoption records, the list goes on and on. One of the biggest concerns of privacy rights groups is that it is becoming increasingly easier for *other* people to obtain information on you than it is for you to get access to your *own* records. It is estimated that the largest federal agencies and departments maintain over 2000 databanks, and other government entities down to the local level maintain their own. The opportunity to make a little extra money selling personal information about you is too tempting to local and state governments especially. Today, the revenue available is too much to pass up. Most people aren't so worried about the fact that the government keeps a lot of records on them, but that these records are being sold or given away to everyone else. You can at least take advantage of a 1997 law and contact your state DMV to opt-out of allowing your vehicle records from being sold to direct marketers (but most people don't).

Federal agencies have even been known to act outside the law knowing that they can get away with it, recording computer output from a distance through the electrical signals they give off, recording conversations or video taping with ultra-sensitive devices developed for the military. The government is very busy gathering information about you and very lax in passing legislation that protects your rights! In some locations, police cameras record license plates of every car passing by. You could even get a ticket for an infraction committed by *someone else* who happens to be driving your car. Speaking of your car, it's easy to attach a location monitoring device and track your driving habits via satellite.

If you delve into the topic of security, surveillance, and espionage, you'll find that governments are *very* paranoid. You can find a list of over 100,000 words and acronyms that the U.S. government scans for on telecommunications including the Internet, phone and fax calls, and email at www.dis.org/erehwon/spookwords.html (also available is a dictionary of acronyms). This site makes reference to the ECHELON system, which constantly searches for these keywords in communications made world wide, primarily by non-military targets such as individuals, governments, companies, and organizations. The ECHELON system works by indiscriminately intercepting very large quantities of communications and then feeding it into super-computers which filter out what is valuable using artificial intelligence aids like Memex to find key words. These key words may be such things as bomb, IRA, gun, or satellite. It would be entirely possible for example, for a mother to be on the phone to a friend describing her son's performance in a school play by saying that he had bombed, and this conversation could then be picked up and investigated as a possible source of terrorist activity. Later, the family's house is burglarized, documents are obviously examined and the computer stolen or compromised, but no one is ever caught. No one ever suspects that the FBI is just *doing its duty*. Much of the information gathered is targeted to keep track of potential terrorists, but there is also a lot of economic intelligence gathering, especially with regard to those countries participating in the GATT negotiations.

ECHELON is operated jointly by five spy organizations under the umbrella of the 1948 UKUSA signals intelligence (SIGNET) agreement. These five SIGNET agencies are the National Security Agency (NSA) in the U.S., Communications Security Establishment (CSE) in Canada, Government Communications Headquarters (GCHQ) in England, Defense Signals Directorate (DSD) in Australia, and Government Communications Security Bureau (GCSB) in New Zealand. As the senior member, NSA effectively runs the show and determines policies. Within Europe, all email, telephone and fax communications are routinely intercepted. The target information is transferred through the strategic hub of London and then by satellite to Fort Meade in Maryland via the hub at Menwith Hill in the North York Moors of the UK. ECHELON uses the Intelsat satellites which are used to transfer most of the world's satellite phone calls, Internet, email, faxes and telexes. Whistleblowers have reported that the NSA has routinely targeted such organizations as Amnesty International, Greenpeace, and Christian Aid. Spying on these organizations has nothing to do with tracking crime and everything to do with suppressing critics of government policies. A similar system called Enfopol is currently being developed in Europe.

In the U.S. less than 0.2 per cent of all wiretap requests during the past decade were related to bombs, arson, or guns, according to an ACLU report called Big Brother in the Wires, Wiretapping in the Digital Age, published in March of 1998. The report states that 83 per cent of all wiretaps, however, were related to gambling and drug offenses. Still, the government wants to strengthen it's ability to snoop on its citizens. Even with over 2 million wiretaps in 1997, the government thinks it needs more. Right now the NSA is pressuring ALL manufacturers of communication devices to make them easy to monitor, leaving back doors in the technology which allow the spy agency to eavesdrop on your communications without your knowledge. This takes the form of components embedded into switches and routers required for Internet connections, devices in cellular phones allowing them to be traced, and chips in personal computers like the recently announced Intel Pentium III which contains a built-in ID that can be read over the Internet. You ARE a criminal aren't you? The government does have a right to listen in on everything you say doesn't it? There's no possible way that something you say could be misconstrued is there? We don't really have to worry about squashing public dissent or threatening unpopular viewpoints in this land of the free! Do we? There really was no conspiracy in the assassinations of Martin Luther King and John F. Kennedy was there?

You might expect that any criminal activity is public record, but seeing your records, if you have any, has in the past usually required that you at least go down to a courthouse or Department of Public Safety and provide proper identification, even a fingerprint, to show that you are looking at your own records. Recently however, in a move to raise revenue, agencies have been increasingly putting criminal records on the Internet. The state of Texas has joined those that allows anyone to see conviction records of anyone in the state for a mere $3.15. They have admitted that there could easily be errors, incomplete information, or inaccuracies for several reasons, including bogus physical identifiers to alias names and numeric identifiers.

The government not only uses intelligence to try to stop terrorism, but it also snoops on the financial transactions of individuals and businesses around the world. There exists a quasi-secret government agency called FinCEN, Financial Crimes Enforcement Network. Launched by the Treasury Department in April 1990, FinCEN is the U.S. government's, and perhaps the world's, most effective financial crime investigation unit. Even Russian President Boris Yeltsin asked for its help in locating stolen Communist Party funds. This state-of-the-art snooping agency operates quietly under the auspices of the Treasury Department. Its mission is to track dirty money, be it the laundered profits from drug sales, money stolen from the failed S&L's, hidden political slush funds, or terrorist cash. FinCEN is newly located near the CIA in Vienna, Virginia, sometimes referred to as Spook City. Inside, agents from the IRS, FBI, DEA, CIA, NSA, Secret Service, custom service, and the post office pool their efforts and information. This includes intelligence gathered from the above-mentioned ECHELON system.

Even now FinCEN is considering adding DTS (Deposit Tracking System) to is list of services available. This would make all of the bank deposit records of anyone in the country available to thousands of police and state or federal bureaucrats, at the touch of a button. FinCEN also has a secretive $2.4 million contract with the U.S. Department of Energy's Los Alamos National Laboratory to develop a powerful money flow model. Unlike FinCEN's current system, Los Alamos's artificial intelligence software will look for unexplained, atypical money flows. The system could perform real-time monitoring of the entire U.S. electronic banking system. This means that all of your banking could be monitored immediately at the time of the transaction. Even without this, the FDIC has recently instructed banks to implement a Know Your Customer profiling campaign that would require bank employees to become amateur cops, always looking suspiciously at your bank transactions to detect any unusual behavior. They are supposed to develop a profile on each customer that would include normally expected deposits, withdrawals, and other transactions. Any deviations would be reported to government agencies for further investigation. Does this sound like Big Brother to you? The FDIC received over 200,000 complaints regarding this program and abandoned it. Still their attitude is that they didn't package or promote it right and the public just needs to be educated about its benefits. It doesn't matter though, currently 85% of all U.S. banks already have a "Know Your Customer" program in operation and report nearly everything to the government on a regular basis.

Since FinCEN is so closely integrated with the CIA and this agency is supposedly prohibited from spying on U.S. citizens, a problem arises when it comes to tracking all the financial transactions of regular citizens. The CIA has admitted that they spied on U.S. citizens for years, but promised that they stopped in the 1970's (you do believe them don't you?). Civil liberties groups even now have serious doubts about their truthfulness and fear that they would find some way to download, copy, or otherwise secretly access this bank data. Some folks connected to the CIA even now admit that this data could easily be used for blackmail, bribery, and extortion. Bruce Hemmings, a veteran CIA clandestine-services officer who retired in 1989 has reported that the CIA routinely digs for financial dirt on people from whom the agency wants specific information. These people are typically foreign intelligence officers working in the U.S. in diplomatic missions. It has been suggested that even our Senators and House representatives are easily intimidated by the potential of an FBI search of their personal lives, especially their finances, and can be swayed by suggestions concerning their vulnerability.

DTS and FinCEN could easily be used for quieting unwanted dissent or inquiries into questionable operations of intelligence agencies (or reducing their budgets) by congressional leaders. In fact, many people see FinCEN as a catalyst for a powerful, all-seeing, all-knowing, global financial tracking organization that records data on the entire world. Working in conjunction with some powerful political leaders and other corporate officials, everyone's life could be controlled by rules set forth from a few posh offices in London and New York. Any financial problems the banks might encounter would be easily remedied by taxes imposed on citizens everywhere and flowing through from government agencies to the Federal Reserve and then to the banks. Even today, FinCEN is working closely with INTERPOL in Europe. Remember, you pay for the CIA, FinCEN, and all the other intelligence gathering agencies with your tax dollars!

The justification for FinCEN and other related intelligence gathering is usually a combination of the following:

- Tracking terrorist activities or their finances
- Tracking drug dealers and their money
- Tracking white collar crime, like that involved in the S&L loan scandal
- Identifying and freezing assets kept in this country by "enemies" of the U.S.

The GAO has audited FinCEN and given it a clean bill of health, but it curiously fails to mention any concerns about privacy, civil liberties, or the appropriate role of the intelligence community with regard to law-abiding citizens. There are legitimate concerns regarding privacy, a ranking House banking committee staffer conceded in an interview with *Wired*. Quite frankly, there hasn't been much congressional oversight with respect to the intelligence community's involvement with FinCEN. When you start trying to look into this, you start running up against all kinds of roadblocks. The GAO official involved in auditing FinCEN agreed that privacy concerns haven't been addressed.

Gateway is a pilot program launched in Texas in July of 1998 that gives state and local law enforcement officials direct access to the massive federal Financial Database (FDB) through a designated FinCEN coordinator. FDB contains the records that financial institutions have been filing under the Bank Secrecy Act for the last 23 years. These contain CTR's (currency transaction reports of amounts over $3,000), suspicious transaction reports, International Transportation of Currency or Monetary Instruments reports, and Foreign Bank and Financial Accounts reports. Congress is also expected to grant FinCEN authority to tap into the database of Forms 8300, which are reports of payments over $10,000 received in a trade or business. These documents principally contain information on deposits, withdrawals, and the movement of large sums of currency. Reportedly FinCEN intends to give all state governments individual access to the FDB.

State coordinators designated by FinCEN would have access to the system, as FinCEN is uncomfortable with giving 50,000 federal agents and 500,000 police officers direct electronic access to its database. This is very sensitive information, concedes Andy Flodin, special assistant to the FinCEN director. How long it would take to eliminate this restriction is hard to say, but the information would be so desirable that you can bet it would be sooner rather than later.

While the FDB contains only records on major money movements, the Deposit Tracking System (DTS) is potentially much more intrusive. If implemented, the estimated $12.5 million computer system could be used to penetrate the security of bank accounts belonging to you, me, and 388 million other bank account holders in the US. The government argues that such a system is necessary for two reasons: first, to adequately assess the funding needed for federal deposit insurance and second, to locate the assets of individuals ordered by courts to make restitution for financial crimes like the ones who made off with billions in the savings and loan debacle (most of which has not yet been recovered). You do accept this rationale don't you. Keep in mind that there is always some excuse when the government wants to take away more of your rights. Usually the excuses have something to do with public safety, but are often disguised as ways of streamlining procedures or otherwise saving taxpayers' money.

Many other governmental agencies are also engaged in intelligence gathering. Recently the *Washington Post* issued a report on the Department of Defense's attempt to come up with workable plans for an offensive cyberwar. See details at: http://jya.com/cyber-how.htm. It says that a component of cyberwar offense is regular monitoring of other countries networks and military command systems for the purpose of pre-planning the battlefield. The Department of Defense justifies ignoring the limitations of intelligence agencies' need to get presidential approval for invading the borders of other countries by saying that cyberspace is borderless. They operate many covert programs that are prepared to disrupt foreign operations like the nuclear command and control systems of Pakistan and India should the need arise. They even claim to be able to disable an entire country in six hours by disrupting their electronic infrastructure.

A *Wired* news article on Wednesday, July 29, 1998, reported that a top Pentagon official said in a speech that no two people in the world have a 'God-given right' to communicate outside the reach of prying government ears. The comments were made by Deputy Secretary of Defense John Hamre to a gathering of Fortune 500 corporate information officers. He confirmed that military officials were in discussions with Netscape Communications to create trap doors for government and military eavesdroppers. These trap doors would allow intelligence agencies to listen in on any Internet communications occurring on service providers' equipment located in this country. Russia already has admitted that its government does this.

If you expect your representatives in Washington to come to your aid in the war against credit and identity theft or for them to protect your privacy and rights, think again! A report by a Washington public interest group says the real problem is that lawmakers accept campaign money from corporations that want access to people's personal information. In a study by The Center for Public Integrity, Congress was found to be highly influenced by contributions from banks, health care, insurance and credit companies that lobby for continued access to personal data. Congress seems to have substantially aided and abetted the invaders of privacy, not the public," said Charles Lewis, director of the center. The financial services industry gave $32 million to congressional candidates during the 1995-96 election, with hospitals, health-maintenance organizations and pharmaceutical companies giving $13 million more, said the center, a nonpartisan research group based in Washington. The Center found that the founder of CDB Infotek of Santa Ana, Calif., Rick Rozar, gave $100,000 to the Republican National

Committee in October of 1997. The company provides a person's full name, birth date and Social Security, telephone and driver's license numbers for $7. So now you know "the rest of the story".

Big business

Contests, sweepstakes, free giveaways, warranty and product registrations, blood drives, clerks asking for names, addresses, phone numbers when making a purchase, surveys, charitable giving, credit card purchases, subscriptions to periodicals, mail order purchases, compiling file and directory names in your computer during an online registration or purchase are all ways that corporations are gathering information about you. Companies regularly buy lists from clubs, organizations, churches, and telemarketers. Lists are sold and resold dozens of times. Even when you answer an ad, but don't buy anything, information about you is being compiled. What do you think mail-in rebates are for? You can probably get the item for the same price elsewhere, without giving up your name to marketers. They want YOU, well actually they want your money, but having just a little information about you is enough, they can sell that to lots of people who are more than willing to pay! Oh you'll get your little rebate all right and a whole lot more, in advertising! Your lifestyle and buying habits are all recorded and sold, along with information about your vacations, reading habits, hobbies, religious affiliation and much more. Nothing about you is too trivial. Everything has a value. You don't have to be rich or famous either.

If you register a complaint against a company for problems with a product or service, your status as a troublemaker may be recorded. If you get on the Internet and complain in usenet chat rooms, your comments may be recorded and examined by the company you're complaining about, then later used against you, even *years* later. If you seek to fight the behavior of a large corporation, you better have deep pockets because they'll last longer paying the lawyers than you will. The only way to win is not to lose in the first place, ie. protect yourself! Even while corporate America is tracking every possible bit of information on you, it jealously guards its own secrets (and crimes), from consumers, competitors, the government, and law enforcement. Note that recently it has been revealed that the cigarette companies regularly communicated through their attorneys to shield information about their research on nicotine in the client/attorney privilege law. Fortunately for everyone, this trick did not work and they were required to divulge these communications in lawsuits brought by the states of Florida and Minnesota. Similarly, large companies are currently lobbying hard to allow them to do their own internal environmental audits (often containing damning information about their ongoing pollution), keeping the results secret from the law and the media.

Keep in mind that businesses exist to make money. If you don't think they can and will use confidential information against you and for their benefit, consider the following cases also revealed by The Center for Public Integrity in an *Associated Press* report:

The large drugstore chain, CVS Corp., in February of 1997, sent a letter to a Rhode Island psychiatrist, asking why one of its employees was being treated with an anti-anxiety drug. CVS later said it conducts reviews of employee treatment to improve the quality of care and "to contain our benefit costs."

A worker at a national laboratory found that her employer had secretly tested her for syphilis, sickle-cell anemia and pregnancy during routine company medical exams. The woman, along with six other co-workers sued the lab and is now negotiating a settlement.

A woman in Orlando, Florida, who went to her doctor for routine tests, was later solicited by a pharmaceutical company that had obtained her medical records. They suggested that she try its new cholesterol medication.

Companies routinely collect, share, sell, and barter your personal records as if they were nothing more than paper clips. Your personal information has a market value, but *you* don't get the benefits of its exchange. Even old newspaper articles have value. Major newspapers have been saving them on disk since 1985 and making them available on the Internet. They can then be searched for keywords, including your name. Scam artists regularly go through obituaries looking for rich widows to offer investments to and to tell them about the great prizes they've won (if they will just send in a hundred dollars for shipping or insurance).

Income tax preparers

You will even find scam artists running legitimate income tax preparation services who later prey on selected customers by selling the financial information to third parties, or later contacting them with phony schemes or investments. The elderly are especially targeted. These scam artists win the confidence of their customers and then pass the name on to associates who do the dirty work. This is even true of volunteers and employees working for the big name groups.

Tax preparers online may be sloppy with your confidentiality even if they are legitimate companies. Only about half of all tax-related sites post a privacy policy, according to a study by Enonymous.com, a company that offers products and services related to Web site privacy. "In general we found 75 percent of Web sites don't post a privacy policy," Enonymous.com founder Tim Kane reported. Tax-related sites with a privacy policy generally rule out selling or sharing customer data but only a few meet Enonymous.com's top criteria of not contacting users without consent. So, Kane said, Enonymous.com rated tax sites as "Good," "Pretty Good," "Bad" and the "Ugly." They found only one site, E-1040, deserved a four-star rating (the best). Among general tax sites, only Fairmark.com received four stars, while the H&R Block site received a three-star rating, meaning it asks for explicit user permission before contacting a visitor, and that it may share personally identifiable information with third parties, with the permission of its visitors. Enonymous gave two-star ratings (they may contact visitors without permission but promise not to share, sell or trade visitor data) to Macintax.com, Quicken.com, Securetax.com and Taxact.com. One-star-rated tax sites often cause their customers to receive unsolicited and unwelcome email and junk postal mail. Among them: Yahoo's tax site, taxes.yahoo.com; Money.com; Armchairmillionaire.com; Tax.org; taxes4less.com; hdvestonline.com; Taxcut.com; and Intuit.com. The Ugly (sites with no privacy policy), include general information sites dtonline.com, naea.org, Taxweb.com, Jacksonhewitt.com, Taxprep1.com and Taxattack.com.

Credit reporting agencies

All credit activity linked to a Social Security or Social Insurance Number or done through American or Canadian banks is reported to the credit reporting agencies, including the identity of entities asking for information about you, and also mistakes, old information, or data on a completely different person (all it takes is a 1 digit error in your SSN). In a study done in 1998 by WashPIRG, whose researchers surveyed 133 credit reports, errors were found in 70% and serious errors, such as false delinquencies or accounts that did not belong to the person were found in 29% of the cases. This information, along with it's errors, is available to anyone with the will or knowledge to get it. If you don't have direct access, you can buy it for about $75.00. It's possible for someone to not only got a credit report on you that lists your credit history, but they can also get an *investigative* credit report that can include hearsay information about character, lifestyle, and reputation garnered from friends, acquaintances, neighbors, fellow workers, or members of associations you belong to. Credit header data is the identifying information that accompanies consumers' credit reports. It consists of name, name variations, address, former addresses, telephone number (even unlisted numbers if known), date of birth (usually limited to month and/or year of birth) and Social Security Number. Although credit header information is generated as part of the credit reporting process, the Federal

Trade Commission has not been limiting its dissemination under the Fair Credit Reporting Act. Consequently, credit header data is sold separate from the credit history and has become the mainstay of a number of people-finding services provided by information vendors such as CDB Infotek, Lexis-Nexis, Information America and IRSC. On Aug. 26, 1998, however, an administrative law judge, presiding over a six-week administrative trial at the FTC, wrote a decision that Trans Union, the only bureau selling header info was invading consumers' privacy when it furnished it to anyone except under specific circumstances. Trans Union, who makes a lot of money selling this information to a wide variety of customers, vowed to appeal using a free speech argument. Do you get along with everyone? Might there ever be someone who may have a reason to say something slightly negative about you (or draw erroneous conclusions about something you did)? Do you know what is on your report?

Insurance and health related organizations

Car, life, health, and homeowners insurance companies keep records that may include life style information. All of your medical records are easily found and dissected for excuses to deny you insurance or claims. HMO's are making it even easier. In addition, some companies call acquaintances, fellow employees, employers, neighbors, or even people just living in the same town to find out *pertinent* information about you (which of course may or may not be true). They want a profile on you. There was a case in Maryland in which a large bank was able to get the names of cancer patients from the state health commission and revoke the loans of those who matched! Sara Lee had planned to collaborate with Lovelace Health Systems, a subsidiary of Cigna Insurance Co., to match employee health records with work-performance reports to find workers who might benefit from antidepressants. Keep in mind that at least a third of all Fortune 500 companies regularly review health information before making hiring decisions. Will they also start

DNA screening, looking for genetic weaknesses? There are already reports of discrimination based on genetic testing! Insurance companies would like to have DNA samples of everyone to be able to screen for possible diseases or genetic weaknesses. They would then obviously refuse to cover individuals with those problems, or charge them exorbitant rates. This scenario plays out even though the person may never develop any of the potential diseases or conditions. A genetic weakness in your parent could prevent you and any of your children or children's children forever down the line, from receiving health insurance. Lets take a look at what is already known, even without this DNA sampling.

What is included in your medical records?

- *Identification sheet* - listing your name, address, phone Number, insurance type and policy number, and probably your Social Security Number.
- *Problem list* - including a list of all significant illnesses, conditions, or surgeries.
- *Medication record* - listing all prescriptions and possibly any medication allergies.
- *History and Physical* - document describing major illnesses and surgeries, family history of diseases, your health habits, current medications, height, weight, blood pressure, pulse, respiration, and any symptoms.
- *Progress Notes* - made by doctors, nurses, therapists, social workers, or technicians providing care to you and including their reflections on your responses to treatment, their observations, and plans for further treatment.
- *Consultation* - the opinion of a physician other than your primary care physician.
- *Physician's Orders* - contained in a document that has your doctor's directions for other members of your medical team regarding your medications, tests, diet, treatments, or therapy.

- *Imaging and X-ray Reports* - describing any X-ray results, mammograms, ultrasounds, or scans.
- *Electrocardiogram* - (ECC, EKG) report on your heart condition.
- *Lab Reports* - describing the results of tests conducted on body fluids, including blood, sputum, and urine. A complete blood work-up report may be contained in the report, but your blood type is usually not included.
- *Immunization Record* - listing immunizations to such diseases as polio, diphtheria, pertussis, tetanus, measles, mumps, rubella, and influenza. You should have your own record of these for schools which may require them before entrance.
- *Correspondence* - exchanged between you and your healthcare provider, inquiries made by insurance companies, and copies of any forms your physician has completed and sent at your request.
- *Authorization Forms* - including copies of consent for admission, treatment, surgery, and release of information.
- *Additional Reports* - may include Hospital Discharge Summaries, Graphic Sheets, Recovery Room Records, Pathology Reports, Anesthesia Reports, and Operative Reports.

If you see areas in the above reporting procedures that might be open to interpretation or misunderstanding, you are not alone. Notes, comments, opinions, conclusions, and outright hearsay might all contain untrue, incomplete, or unflattering information about you. Even the highly respected Center for Disease Control is behind gathering information about you, whether it is accurate or not. It has encouraged state health agencies to build databases based on immunization records which would include data similar to the above. These files would be kept on all children and be a basis for a national medical dossier. The citizens and legislature of Texas found out about this and objected, but the Department of Health circumvented new rules limiting the gathering of data by requiring parental consent and went ahead anyway, ordering the filing of information based on *assumed* parental consent.

Banks

The big banks may complain about being over-regulated, but believe me, they are very good team players with the government in regulating and tracking your financial life! Your bank is required to report any cash transaction over $3000.00 or any movement of funds over $10,000.00. Tellers and officers are told to report any *suspicious* activity and they can even receive a reward for helping to catch someone. Money laundering is now defined in over 150 ways and has become a catchall for the IRS and other government agencies who may have some reason to target you. Your money can be confiscated with only a suspicion and getting it back could take years if you ever get it back at all!

If you deal in large amounts of cash, you are assumed to be a drug dealer. Actually banks, big businesses and the government hate cash. Governmental and banking regulations make it increasingly difficult to conduct business on a cash basis. Trying to move it is even more difficult. Did you know that you can be arrested (and your money confiscated) if you try to carry more than $10,000 out of the country without reporting it? There are some sad stories of innocent people who tried, not knowing the regulations. They had worked hard and legitimately for years, saving up money to bring back to relatives in their native country, only to be accosted by border guards or airport agents accusing them of being drug dealers, then confiscating all of their money. Money sniffing dogs detected it in their bags! Big business is madly trying to eliminate this antiquated means of money exchange because it is much more difficult to obtain a fee on a transaction conducted with cash.

Along with recording the details of the transaction, including taking pictures of both sides of all checks (very handy for tracking where the funds are going), your picture is usually taken too. ATM machines take your picture whenever you use them. You are recorded on video tape whenever you walk into a bank or even enter the parking lot. Swiss banks take pictures of all people who enter the building and keep them for archival purposes. These photos have been useful in convicting people for money laundering.

Just remember that most local banks will reveal all to just about any governmental agency and can be tricked into disclosing your financial affairs to a good investigator too. Even buying a cashiers check to pay a bill anonymously may require that you provide ID and will require a remitter's name (hint - use money orders).

Political organizations and extremist groups

These groups do their own data searches and record keeping. The Republican National Committee is one of the worst offenders at failing to remove names from its mailing lists, even after multiple requests. All political parties however regard their mailing lists as one of their most valuable possessions. They can get names of all registered voters and their voting records, in addition to their financial status or neighborhood so that they can target people with specific literature or requests. Consistent givers are solicited repeatedly. Some fringe groups may even do surveillance on you or track your membership in other organizations. A group's records may be used by the FBI or the IRS to track people and gather information in ways that would not be legal by a government entity. The data is later made available when it appears *accidentally* in a private residence of an agent or police officer. There are groups who target ethnic or religious organizations, environmentalists, abortion rights or equal rights advocates, and just about every other type of individual, organization, or movement you can think of. If you have any doubts about the power of a determined individual or group, note the following article in the *Washington Times*, April 16, 1998:

> Senior Pentagon leaders were stunned by a military exercise showing how easy it is for hackers to cripple U.S. military and civilian computer networks, according to new details of the secret exercise. Using software obtained easily from hacker sites on the Internet, a group of National Security Agency officials could have shut down the U.S. electric-power grid within days and rendered impotent the command-and-control elements of the U.S. Pacific Command.

If hackers could do this much damage to our country's infrastructure, do you really think it would be difficult for them to rearrange your credit or medical records? It is well known that many extremist groups advocate the use of bombing, assassination, extortion, and other violent means to further their causes. Having your name in the paper or on the news may subject you to reprisals from one of these groups if they can easily get your address and phone number (and of course they can!).

Employers/employees

Video surveillance cameras and listening devices are everywhere including rest rooms. Email is recorded and read both by employers and anyone else in cyberspace who wants to pick it up. Your conversations may be recorded along with your Internet visits. Employers can even record the number of keystrokes per hour and idle keyboard time. Fellow employees may be interrogated about your character and you wouldn't even know it. If employers look into your data files and find something they don't like, you could be a target of someone who just doesn't like the church you go to, and courts tend to rule in favor of the employer. Do you know what is contained on your employee ID tag?

Employers, how well do you trust your payroll personnel? Is everyone honest? Have you done background checks? It's so easy to steal data from *any* department for sale to competitors, its almost a joke. I am constantly amazed at how lax security is in most companies. Your data processing people have access to the life of your business with the ability to steal company secrets and then set up shop themselves as your competitor. Do you use encryption for sensitive documents, product designs, strategies, etc.? Do you encrypt your email? Do you routinely throw away all kinds of sensitive printed information without shredding it? How do you know that the janitors are only working for *your* firm?

Schools

In addition to extensive information on you within school records, your children are also encouraged to spy on you and report any potential "abuse". Parents have found out only accidentally that spying was going on when their children mentioned assignments with questions such as: "Do you ever feel unloved at home?" "Are there any things you would change about your parents if you could?" There are cases going on right now in which children were threatened and coerced into lying to police or school authorities in order to prosecute parents who happened to disagree with these same authorities (or belonged to an organization out of favor with the authorities). You won't be warned either, your children can be taken away before you even have a chance to talk with them or defend yourself. Then you have to go to the trouble and expense of proving your innocence. On the college level, reunion committees are a favorite of private investigators for tracking down deadbeats. It seems that people just can't resist telling all to the committee chairman or including details of activities and important events on those forms that come around regularly (usually also asking for a donation). You're tracked by your student loans too, with payments that usually stretch out for years.

The Internet

Every address you visit may be recorded in your computer's cache memory or log files. Many *sites* also track the locations of visitors. Government stings are set up to lure unsuspecting people. It is even possible to record and download the contents of your computer during a visit to a web site (especially if you use Microsoft's Internet Explorer with Active-X turned on, Active-X controls have full access to your computer)! There are stories of bogus sites making charges to phones for long distance overseas calls (terminated only when the computer was turned off, not when the user left the site). Cookies record a wide variety of information about you and your computer and can later be read by sites you visit. They are supposedly used to create an electronic passport identifying you to online marketers who can then tailor your viewing and advertising pleasures to your own interests. Posting to news groups definitely leaves a trace of your identity, but even visiting groups can be recorded if there is a perceived need. There are also many interactive sites that encourage children to reveal vital information about their families while innocently playing a game or entering a contest.

Its fairly easy to spoof your email address and use it as an identity to engage in all sorts of communications, including spamming (unsolicited email), which can land you in all sorts of trouble with fellow users who may want to retaliate. Hackers have also been known to not just change web sites (including the FBI, CIA, National Security Agency, and many major corporations), but to secretly use sites as depositories for illicit, illegal, stolen programs or pornographic material (all without the knowledge of the owner of the site).

One thing that is becoming an increasing threat to our privacy is the very convenience of the Internet. Companies like Amazon.com, while selling books or tapes, also sell mailing lists of customer information. Ordering online is very convenient, yet each time we use it, we open ourselves up to someone having access to our personal data. Additionally, as DSL lines and other forms of Internet access become more available (and cheaper), people will tend to leave their computers on and connected to the Internet all the time. This opens the possibility of snoopers gaining access to their hard drives and all the information on them in the middle of the night when it won't be noticed. Microsoft has already admitted that they will record the contents of people's hard drives when they register their software online. If you leave your computer on all the time, it is susceptible to the threat of cyber-snooping through Trojan horse programs that tag along with legitimate downloads, or even what is called push technology which downloads programs to your computer and then runs them without your knowledge. You can purchase programs that automatically connect to the Internet and update web sites or other information you want while you sleep. These programs could contain errors, viruses, or trojan horses.

Companies may even compromise your Internet security through mistakes made on their systems. A Canadian gentleman found his name, electronic mail address and bank account number mistakenly transmitted over the Internet to nearly 500 clients of the Canadian Imperial Bank of Commerce's discount brokerage arm. Hey, accidents happen. Customers have also found that making reservations to hotels or resorts in foreign countries through web sites that look real, were really just ruses to get credit card account numbers.

A fairly serious security bug was discovered in the Microsoft web server, Internet Information Server (IIS) back in July of 1998 (more bugs have subsequently been found). It is reported that someone could expose the details of executable scripts that run on the server, thus potentially exposing confidential details about your network, software, and passwords. A series of fixes and workarounds for various revisions of the server was made available on Microsoft's bug description page, but the question one must ask is, does your company use Microsoft's web server, and if it does, are the people involved in its maintenance and security up on all of the potential threats to its security? You could also ask this of any web site you visit. Hallmark was embarrassed on Valentines Day, when a bug was discovered in its software, allowing names, addresses, phone numbers, and love notes to be accessed by thousands of unauthorized people.

Phone, cable, and utility companies

Would phone companies make available records on all of your phone calls, even those that are not long distance and therefore don't show up on your bill? Sure they would, to the right people! It has been reported that they actually record many calls and archive them for later use by government agencies. The police don't even need a warrant to see a record of your calls. Utility companies also make available information about your electrical usage to law enforcement officials (high users may be drug dealers growing marijuana). Tapping your house or phone is very easy using phony utility repair people or attaching a bug to the outside of the house or to the phone jack leading inside. Fax messages are also easily intercepted and tracked. During a lawsuit, a manager in AT&T's security department affirmed under oath that the company does not have written procedures designed to prevent disclosure of its customers' telephone bills. Your cellular phone calls are also easy to eavesdrop on and your location can be easily determined too.

Cable television is in over half of the nation's homes. The 2-way communications that cable companies use is for the ability of the TV set smartbox to enable (or disable) special services, such as pay per view movies. The original systems relied on the customer calling the cable company, which then would send an authorization key to the entire cable system. If your box matched the key, programming would be descrambled and you would see the picture. The next generation of TV set top boxes communicated back to the cable company, making the telephone call unnecessary, since the information sent back contained both the request for services, as well as the numeric key that identified the box. The newest option, now that the cable companies are getting into the Internet business, allows the transmission of data and other information over the existing cable network. While some of the cable-modems that are being offered do have the ability for two way communication (and also the ability to spy on you), a more typical scenario uses the cable network as the downlink from the Internet, while the upstream information (from computer to the Internet) still uses a telephone line, thus limiting the spying potential to the slower modem connection. It would be possible to hide a camera in a set top box, but the amount of data that would need to be sent precludes this from being practical at this time. Even audio data would require a great deal of bandwidth. As equipment becomes more sophisticated and the connections acquire more capacity however, this could certainly be a scenario for the future.

Common criminals, hackers, and jokers

It seems like nothing is sacred anymore. Garbage picking is very common and not even illegal. Thieves look for receipts or credit card records, then use the numbers (and your signature!) to rack up purchases all over the world. Private investigators use garbage to find dirt on people or to track their whereabouts. Lots of information is available from your garbage, and once it's put outside on the curb, it's public property. Businesses are also a big target of garbage bandits. Again, credit card information or business secrets may command a big price with the right people.

Cell phone cloning and recording of calls is really easy for analog cell phones or cordless phones, all you need is a scanner, available at any electronics store. Baby monitors are also easily picked up by other cordless phones or scanners. Sometimes even children's walkie-talkies pick up conversations. There is a market for these recorded conversations too! Some people just like to listen in for entertainment, others are there to make some money. There's a huge market for cloned cell phones and you can be a target even if you're not talking on the phone.

People don't always work in a job for the sheer enjoyment of it. In 1995 a convicted child rapist working as a technician in a Boston hospital went through a thousand computerized records looking for potential victims. He was caught when a caller ID traced him back to the hospital.

Even mistakes can create havoc. Recently Matt Drudge reported in his email dispatch of the week to over 60,000 readers that a White House aide was a wife beater. He later recanted the story, but the aide is preparing to sue him. A lawsuit won't undo the damage though. Many others have also been victims, including Tommy Hilfiger, falsely accused of racism, Brad Pitt, seen online in the nude, and Kurt Vonnegut, who was accused of giving a commencement speech he never made. Do you get on the Internet and try to prove your innocence? Good luck.

The newspaper may also be a source of information about you. Old people are probably scammed the most. Con artists avidly read obituary pages to spot widows' names, knowing that they often have insurance money or life savings that are potentially vulnerable. Then comes the inevitable call promising all sorts of prizes, services, or products. The <u>least</u> that an elderly person should do is to have an unlisted number! This won't stop the determined con artists, but will make the majority pass on to easier prey.

A 1998 report on ABC news said that over a million women each year are victims of a stalker along with over 300,000 men! Most of the time its by an ex-spouse or lover and often results in violence. These people are determined. If they are prone to act violently, they are also thinking of other ways to make someone's life miserable. One anonymous accusation of child rape can follow you forever, even if it's totally false!

Extortionists and blackmailers also like technology. A recent story out of Argentina reports that the early leader in their 1999 election race claims that extortionists had bugged his phone for years. He says that they then doctored the recordings to discredit his family. Buenos Aires Mayor Fernando De la Rua, of the opposition Radical Party, said conversations were changed to make it appear that his two sons had arranged with university teachers to fake their grades. If you think no one would do this to you, you might consider how much it would be worth to them. The wealthier you are, the more likely a target you become.

Hackers, criminals, and practical jokers love the Internet! Computers hooked up to the Internet either separately or via a network are especially vulnerable if they use Windows 95/98 or Windows NT. A recent article by Bruce V. Bigelow, a *Union Tribune* staff writer, written March 4, 1998 shows how powerful hackers are and the potential for widespread damage that exists. Bigelow reports that on the night Bill Gates was preparing to testify before Congress, someone used the Internet to launch a massive attack against computers running Microsoft NT. This caused machines to crash nationwide. The hackers primarily targeted computers running Windows NT in government and university offices. Craig Huckabee, a research associate in the Computer Systems Laboratory at the University of Wisconsin in Madison said: "In our department, I would have to say about 90 percent of the machines were affected." No one knows the full extent of the attack but similar problems were experienced at the Massachusetts Institute of Technology, Northwestern University, The University of Minnesota and at UC campuses in Berkeley, Irvine, Los Angeles, and San Diego. Unclassified Navy computers connected to the Internet also crashed on Point Loma, in Charleston, S.C., Norfolk, VA, and elsewhere. Victims experience what is called the blue screen of death. Nothing can be done to recover from such a condition and the machines have to be restarted. Any transactions or data in memory at the time is lost.

Computer security experts in San Diego said the incident, known as a denial-of-service attack, was essentially benign. The computers that crashed could be restarted without losing data or otherwise compromising network security. This is not entirely true however, as data in memory may be completely lost depending on the program running at the time of the crash. The attackers used the Internet to widely distribute a snippet of data, known as a network packet, that was deliberately malformed, said Ron Broersma, a civilian computer security expert at the Navy labs on Point Loma. Network packets have to follow certain standards. If you send a packet that doesn't conform, the operating system should catch the flaws and just drop it. Instead, the packet exploited a bug in Windows NT by instructing the computer to devote excessive memory resources to solving a problem that cannot be solved. The story was not even given much media attention, possibly because people running Windows products are so used to their computers crashing. Some experts said the attack may reflect animosity built up towards Microsoft. Some people just want to make Microsoft look bad. Since the attack occurred during the company's hearings on monopolistic practices, it is not surprising.

While destructive hacking like that mentioned above can be prosecuted, you should know that it isn't even illegal, yet, to steal someone's identity. Someone can use another person's credit history, Social Security Number and driver's license information to obtain loans, take over property, and anything else the owner himself could do. Fraud is illegal, but going around calling yourself someone else and using their identity apparently is not. The General Accounting Office released a report on May 26, 1998 finding that cases of identity theft are increasing. The GAO found that no federal agency has primary jurisdiction over the problem and a lack of a clear definition is hampering efforts to track it. Credit bureaus are also largely ignoring the issue, with only one, Trans Union keeping track of consumer inquiries. Its representatives told the GAO that two-thirds of the firm's 522,000 customer inquiries in 1997 involved identify theft!

The single most important item that identifies you is your Social Security or Social Insurance Number. It is a common identifier used by many agencies and businesses and is also frequently used as a password by credit card companies. The

Social Security Administration reported that there were 1153 investigations for Social Security Number misuse in 1997, up from 305 in 1996. The Justice Department reported that it prosecuted over 2000 cases of SSN misuse between 1992 and 1997. The Associated Credit Bureaus, a trade association, told the GAO its members made tens of millions of dollars annually selling information from credit reports to marketers, merchants and others. Because of this huge market in selling personal information and the ease of acquiring it via computers, it is probably unlikely that there will be adequate protection provided by state or federal legislation. You're going to have to take this responsibility on yourself. There's a guy in California who is creating a database of Social Security Numbers. He proposes putting them on sweatshirts and selling them in specialty clothing stores! It's not even illegal, according to the Social Security Administration. You can find Bill Gates' number on the Internet right now. Don't be surprised to find it on someone's T-shirt somewhere soon.

Finally, just so you don't start to think that data theft and unauthorized distribution is relegated to any particular segment of society, consider a recent TV news report that said criminals secretly installed a miniature camera in a gas station in the Toronto suburb of Newmarket. As customers were using debit cards to make payments directly from their bank accounts, their fingers would be videotaped to obtain their secret personal identification numbers. The gas station clerk, who was in on the scam, would provide data from the card reader. A dummy card with a copy of the machine-readable data was then used during midnight trips to ATMs and, armed with the PIN numbers from the videotape, the thieves could easily withdraw the maximum amount. The withdrawals were made at midnight so that the maximum daily amount could be obtained twice on one visit, once before midnight and once after. Three suspects, all from the Toronto area, have been charged. Police say hundreds of thousands of dollars were stolen and that the criminals were planning to expand soon to 5 more gas stations. It is also not uncommon for thieves to use binoculars to watch people use calling cards, especially at airport phone booths. They can pick up the card number and the PIN. Speaking of criminals, it has also been recently reported that prisoners in Texas have been setting up web sites profiling their victims (or victims to be). Isn't it amazing what one can do from prison these days!

Spouses, background checks, & private investigators

In America, half of all marriages end in divorce and ex-spouses can sometimes be very nasty. It's not uncommon to see news articles about old boyfriends or ex-husbands tracking down their former spouses and harming them somehow. It is estimated that over a million women a year are threatened with stalkers. These people can easily hire private investigators to track down the victim, getting the Social Security Number and finding where they live and/or work. It isn't expensive either. Even safe houses are sometimes penetrated. Now there's the Internet stalker, who sends *email* to the victim.

Entire departments of the government also exist solely for the purpose of tracking ex-spouses, supposedly to find those not paying child support. Whether it's a private investigator or a government employee, they have many means at their disposal to find you, and if a national ID system goes into effect, their jobs will be easier stlll. They may even resort to following you to track down your spending habits, recreational pursuits or hidden properties you may own or rent. They may ask for opinions from neighbors or acquaintances about your personal habits or tap your phone. Even your zip code, especially the 9 digit number, gives someone a precise location of where you live (and what kind of neighborhood it's in). Through mail-order catalogues or spy stores, you can purchase equipment that can pick up nearby phone conversations, listen to conversations through a wall, pick up the radiation all computers emit to read their keystrokes or screen images, or listen in on distant conversations from vibrations created by voices on window glass. The first step however, is always to use the phone and computer, looking up your paper trail on vast databases. Once particular identifying information is determined, the rest is relatively easy and personal surveillance is usually not needed.

Private investigators use all sorts of methods, some of which are not legal, to locate people. Pretexts are often used to trick people into giving them information on someone. A private investigator will impersonate the target to get information about where they live, work, or hang out. They may call the person and claim to have a package to deliver, information about a dead or sick relative, or a summons to jury duty. They will call phone companies and claim to be a repairman needing the address of a certain phone number. They may call a former landlord or employer and claim to be a long lost friend or relative or a business that needs to deliver some money to the subject and then ask for the name and address of the person listed as the one to contact in case of emergency.

A determined PI will usually be able to find most anyone. They work for money and may not check out the real reason a customer has for getting information about someone. They may also run real or phony side businesses to use solely for the purpose of obtaining records. For instance, some states will not release driver's license information, so the PI will have stationery printed up with a name like Personnel Verification Corp. and send in a letter requesting driver license/identity card application information for the purpose of a background verification. Back comes the report, often with Social Security Number (depending on the state).

Keep in mind that most PI's are probably hard working, honest people just trying to provide a service to the customer, but the resources available to them and the money making opportunities make the potential for abuse rather high. The following is available to private investigators, law enforcement officers, licensed collection agencies, bounty hunters, bondsmen, law firms employing investigators, or investigative professionals:

pilot license records
consumer credit reports, header and detail
business credit reports
assumed business names
business telephone numbers
corporate officer search by executive's name
corporation records, registered agents, and officers
civil court judgments and filings
sales and franchise tax filings
workmen's compensation filings
bankruptcy filings
telephone number referenced to name and address
address referenced to name and telephone
residential telephone numbers by area code or geographical area
real property by name or location
U.S.P.S change of address records
mail drop identifier
post office box number referenced to name and address
Social Security Number death records
Social Security Number usage
motor vehicle records - by owner, license plate, or vin #
driver license header and record
felony, state and county criminal records
tax lien filings
current occupant and neighbors
new neighbors
voter registration records
personal biographical data
financial assets
current employer
television transcripts
mention of someone's name in large newspapers

Databases available from one company are estimated to now contain records for approximately 92% of the adult residents of the United States. More than one billion exact age records are now contained in their databases. A full nationwide search is available to members for $1.00. Each record typically provides name, address, telephone number and date of birth, and is searchable by ANY input criteria - even by a first name. It is possible to search within a specific state, or nationwide. Many state's databases also provide additional vital data, such as driver license numbers. The databases are also linked with a variety of Social Security Number and credit databases allowing a link of selected records to header information. Archived records are reportedly not purged, so that old and possibly inaccurate or incomplete information is kept indefinitely. The databases on nearly everyone are so extensive that in some respects it surpasses that available even to law enforcement. They advertise that even post office box addresses are included in hundreds of thousands of cross-referenced listings.

Here is a very simple and commonly used method to find someone quickly. Let's assume you only have a person's name and state of residence. First you request a copy of their basic identification file from the state Department of Motor Vehicles using an alpha search (almost everyone has a driver's license). You can also get driving records from the DMV that lists all tickets, accidents, etc. This is what insurance companies do to find people to solicit. The DMV is considered a soft touch when it comes to getting information. Why? They make money from fees required for the searches. Departments in 3 states have even sold their pictures to a company in New Hampshire to use in an anti-fraud program (sponsored by the Secret Service). Next, you take the address and phone number data and check to see if it's current using a local phone directory. If the phone number is good (call the person and see if it is, ask for them and see if they will identify themselves), you still need the address. You merely go to a telephone locator directory to find the address for that phone number (this directory is arranged by phone number). If you have an address and need the phone number, you'd use a crisscross directory which lists all numbers on any given street, even the non-published ones! If you need still more information, you could consult what's called a City

Directory. This lists not only phone and address data, but also employment, spouses, children, and a lot more. These directories are available at your local library so you don't even have to buy them. You can request that your name be removed from the crisscross directories sold by Haines & Company and R.L. Polk & Co. by writing to them, but you'll probably have to do this yearly to make sure that your name doesn't reappear.

Haines & Company, Inc.
Criss-Cross Directory
Attn. Director of Data Processing
8050 Freedom Ave., NW
N. Canton, OH 44720
(800) 562-82262

R.L. Polk & Co.
Attn: List Suppression File
26955 Northwestern Highway
South Field, MI 48034
(810) 728-7000

Paper trails lead PI's directly to your door. The following are the most commonly used:

credit card charges
bank checks and statements
wire transfers
phone records
hotel charges and phone records
delivery services
travel agency records
frequent flyer awards
passports
news articles

Retail stores

Price scanners can link your purchases with your credit or ATM card and then pass the information on to others who may purchase the lists and send you junk mail. Retail stores also have lots of contests and giveaway promotions, usually wanting at least your name and address. There are also special privilege cards, memberships, and everything imaginable to get your personal information for marketing purposes. Video cameras are everywhere, recording thieves and everyone else. They are in the rest rooms, in the changing rooms, and, of course, on the display floor. They aren't even illegal in the restrooms or changing rooms if they are used "for security". Even if you never go into a retail store, your picture is being taken on the streets and in parking lots (and garages). You're recorded by surveillance cameras an average of 20 times a day if you live or work in New York City. Your prescriptions are also tracked, giving potential insurance companies or employers information about your medical or mental condition (and where you are).

Free events and services

Blood pressure or cholesterol screenings, blood drives and other free health services collect data on participants. The blood you give could be analyzed for DNA or the presence of any type of virus. Insurance companies are very interested in getting their hands on this information, especially if they could find out that you might have a genetic weakness for some disease or condition. Scam artists of phony investment schemes often look for prospects by visiting churches, country clubs, or senior-citizen centers. There they may offer some kind of service or information on living wills, free tax help, etc. that lure the members into going farther, filling out registration cards for phony giveaways, trips, or more services. After they gain their confidence and their personal information, they come back with fraudulent investments or other schemes at a later time.

This information is also commonly sold to scam artists around the country. Lists may be sold and resold many times, especially if they contain names of people who are taking the bait and falling for the schemes.

Delivery services

UPS now has electronic versions of thousands of people's signatures and it has been suggested that they may be marketable. As of the date of this printing, there are no laws to prevent this from happening. You could refuse to sign for your packages, but you might encounter less hassles if you just don't sign your name or be very sloppy so that the signature cannot be identified.

Even the local pizza delivery may be revealing your address to people who you may not wish to know it. If you call up and tell them your name and/or phone number they will often give out the address if you ask for it, and without verifying who you are! The same goes for airport shuttle services. This may be especially serious if you are being stalked or harassed by a former spouse. Ask them to refrain from giving out personal information without confirming your identity.

II. Personal Information and Your Identity

Personal information ownership

Just who owns all the data stored on you anyway? Do you have a right to have it destroyed, changed, or corrected? Who is to determine the truth about what is correct? Do you *own* the information or even your own *identity*? Even more important, who should or does control it? Is anyone protecting it from abuse? Don't count on the government. State and federal laws are about 50 years behind technology. Besides, the government is one of the worst offenders. Back a hundred years ago, events were generally only recorded on paper or in someone's memory. Both of these things were subject to eventual loss or death. With the advent of computers however, that same information can be reproduced and kept indefinitely. Something that happened to you once when you were a child and had little or no importance even then, can be dredged up and used against you years later.

The U.S. Constitution doesn't expressly grant a right to privacy, but the Supreme Court has interpreted several sections of the Constitution to protect aspects of individual privacy:

The First Amendment's freedom of association and expression clause

The Fifth Amendment's privilege against self-incrimination

Inferences from the Bill of Rights and the Ninth Amendment

II. Personal Information and Your Identity

The Fourteenth Amendment's guarantee of ordered liberty

The strongest protections arise from the Fourth Amendment, which safeguards American citizens, and their places, papers, and effects, from unreasonable searches and seizures. The Supreme Court's interpretations of the Fourth Amendment have some weaknesses however, which allow all kinds of nefarious information gathering and dispersal. Consumers are often asked either online, in a check box, or in person, to sign lengthy disclaimers before they are eligible to receive a service or a benefit. Although these disclaimers purport to protect privacy, many of them contain fine-print provisions that actually waive all the signer's rights.

In Canada, another supposedly "free" country, the Charter of Rights and Freedoms does not specifically speak of privacy protections, but the Supreme Court of Canada has tended to interpret privacy as a basic right.

How did we get into this mess? Part of the problem started back 60 years ago when Social Security was first passed and people were assigned their magical numbers, which of course were only to be used for social security retirement purposes and not for ID. Who owns that card and the number? Look on the back! It clearly states that it's owned by the Social Security Administration and must be returned upon request. Put this book down now and call your local office of the Social Security Administration. Ask them one simple question. Is a Social Security Number mandatory or voluntary? Almost everyone (including a lot of members of Congress!) thinks it is mandatory even though it is not, and almost everyone has one! Try to get a job or a loan without one. If having the number is voluntary, could you use a different number for ID? Sure you can, but being able to use it is another matter. You have the right to have any name or ID number that you establish for yourself. As an American citizen you do not have to use your Social Security Number unless you're asking for government benefits, like disability or food stamps. You were probably assigned the number as a child anyway, and, as it established a contract between you and the Social Security Administration when you were a minor, it really should be considered null and void, since minors cannot by law enter into contractual relationships.

Believe it or not, a strong push for a national ID comes from an international treaty, namely the GATT agreement. Note the following conversation regarding it between Senator Pete Domenici and Senator Pat Moynihan:

> 1994, GATT implementing legislation, Senate debate:
> Senator Pete Domenici:
> "A final question of special concern is that GATT requires that every United States citizen receive an identification number at birth..."
>
> Senator Pat Moynihan:
> "It is the Social Security Number."
> Senator Pete Domenici:
> "The Social Security Number, that is right."
> (C. R., Pg. S15274-S15275, 1994)

In addition, UNICEF is complaining that 40 million babies are born each year around the world without being "registered". The organization says that this means they then fail to qualify for medical care, schooling, vaccinations, and other government benefits. It's position of course is that ALL babies be given an identifying number at birth so that governments can plan for their needs. Nothing is said about privacy concerns or the ability of governments to brand, then discriminate against, certain categories or classes of citizens as is done in many countries today.

Too bad it's not just the fault of the Social Security Administration and international treaties. We ourselves are at fault when we freely give out personal information to just about anyone who asks for it! We join clubs, enter contests, answer surveys, send or call for information ... the list goes on and on.

Our lifestyles reveal everything about us and everything is recorded. Even as we voluntarily use Social Security Numbers, we also do something else every year that is purely voluntary. We file an income tax return! Put this book down again and call your local IRS office. Ask them a very simple question. Is filing an income tax return voluntary for an American citizen? They will tell you that it is, but don't take my word for it. Call them. Now if its voluntary, why do we all send in a complicated form to them each year detailing minute details of our financial life? And, keep in mind, that we do it with a Social Security Number that is also voluntary! The IRS manual on Tax Protestors states that people misunderstand the meaning of the word voluntary. The manual states that the code really means that citizens can volunteer to figure their own tax instead of the government doing it for them, but that filing and paying is not voluntary (only figuring out how much to pay is). Well the Supreme Court doesn't agree with them, but they figure that its their job is to collect the money, not decide on the law. Our tax system is based upon voluntary assessment and payment and not upon distraint Flora v. U.S., 362 U.S. 145. The same is true in Canada, which also has a voluntary system. To be anything *but* voluntary would actually be unlawful.

If you want to blame someone for the fact that everything about you is easily known to the rest of the world, you're going to have to take some responsibility for it yourself! By the way, when you file that income tax return and send in your money, you are dealing with one of the most mismanaged, abusive, irresponsible, and wasteful government agencies in existence today. The *Associated Press* reported in July 1998, that internal audits showed that one in every four seizures the IRS conducted was wrong! It's commonly known that if you go to 100 different CPA's and have your taxes done by them using the exact same information, you will get 100 different returns and tax liabilities. The same thing happens if you ask the same question on a tax matter to 100 different IRS advisors. You are voluntarily sending intimate details of your financial life to these people every year! The IRS also estimates that an average return for someone itemizing deductions may take over 20 hours to prepare in 1999. By the way, I'm not going to get into the debate about whether the income tax applies to you or not. There are many knowledgeable people who are arguing it in court and I will be glad to let them do their job. My job is to inform you of your rights and ways you can protect yourself from people both in and out of the government who have designs on your money and your assets.

Let's move on to corporate America. We don't want to just beat up on the government! A new trade has been created since the dawn of the personal computer and the Internet, namely that of Internet searcher or Information Professional, which even has its own group, the Association of Independent Information Professionals. It is possible for these people to find out just about everything about you, starting with no more than your name, with only a couple of hours on their computers. Carole Lane writes about these new professionals in her book *Naked in Cyberspace: How to Find Personal Information Online*. A company calling themselves 1800ussearch which you can find on the Internet, advertises the following:

Family Security Search
FIND OUT WHAT ANYONE CAN FIND OUT ABOUT EVERY MEMBER OF YOUR FAMILY.

We will conduct extensive National Public Record Database Searches to extract any and all information pertaining to each of your family members. The information you will receive will include a combination of the following:

AKA's (Also Known As)
Alias's
Drivers License Information
Vehicle Ownership
Bankruptcies
Property Ownership
UCC Files

Pilots License
Aircraft Ownership
Deed Transfer Information
Neighbors Phone Listings
Current and Previous Addresses (Up to 20 Years)
Address Profiles
Current and Previous Telephone #'s
Judgements
Corporate Affiliations
Relatives
D.O.B., Drivers License Information
Addresses and Phone #'s

They will also search out adoption records, find out if someone else is using your Social Security Number, and do background checks. They require either a first and last name plus Social Security Number, first and last name and exact date of birth, or a first and last name and previous address. If you don't know an exact date of birth, they say that they can probably help you anyway. They do not warrant that any of the information is correct and disclaim any responsibility for any use the information is put to by buyers of their services. The family search costs $199.95. The background check is $99.95. The last time I checked they had over 100,000 hits on their web page. There are also many other such services available to anyone who wishes to pay the cost.

Some propose a new government agency on privacy to help protect us and decide on our rights, but others suggest that this would only make matters worse and the government should be reduced, not enlarged. What we need is more knowledge, about who's watching us and what we can do about it. Remember that all important Social Security Number. It's currently used as your international ID and you leave a paper trail everywhere you go, all based on the transactions tied to that number. Actually transactions can also be traced even if they are not connected to your Social Security Number if your name, address, and phone number are attached. If the transaction has any data that links you to it, an investigation can follow the links back to you. There are privacy laws that have been enacted to help protect our rights, but they are pretty weak and for the most part ineffectual when it comes to hiding your identity or affairs from a determined investigator. You can see if your state has enacted laws in various categories by looking at the following web site:

www.epic.org:80/privacy/consumer/states.html

You'll have to check further into the specific laws covering the area you're interested in to find if there's any real protection for you since sometimes having a law is worse than not having one.

There are many legislative efforts that involve privacy while enabling the government to fight crime. Among them are:

Wiretap Act
ECPA
CALEA (Communications Assistance for Law Enforcement Act)
Cable Communications Policy Act
Telephone Consumer Protection Act
Fair Credit Reporting Act
Bank Secrecy Act
Right to Financial Privacy Act
Debt Collection Act
Privacy Act
HIPAA (medical privacy)
Video Privacy Protection Act
Various FTC Rulings

The Communications Assistance for Law Enforcement Act, for example, passed in 1994, was supposed to ensure that new technologies and services did not interfere with law enforcement wiretapping. While Congress sought to limit the FBI's control over the telephone system and to strengthen privacy protections, the FBI has attempted to dominate the implementation process by insisting that companies include in their systems features that would give the government more comprehensive surveillance capabilities. You should be extremely wary of the government's intentions with regard to anything that has to do with privacy. The government has shown that it is more interested in intruding on your privacy than it is with protecting it. Note the following:

The National ID

If you're concerned about being branded, numbered, and controlled by corporate or government bureaucrats, and think nothing can be done, take heart. Demonstrating the power of grassroots activism, a coalition of organizations from both the left and the right were able to defeat New Jersey's Gov. Christie Todd Whitman's AccessNJ driver's license proposal in June of 1998 after a massive media and legislative blitz. Headed by the League of American Families and the American Civil Liberties Union of New Jersey, the coalition included the American Family Association, Concerned Women for America, the Conservative Caucus of NJ, and the New Jersey Family Policy Council. The AccessNJ proposal would have created a 10-year smart card drivers license that would have been required for all government programs and services, as well as authorizing banks, hospitals, schools, libraries, credit card and insurance companies to electronically store information on the driver's license. Coalition groups opposed this measure as an invasion of personal privacy because of the lack of guarantees by administration officials about how the information would be used and by whom. ACLU-NJ staff attorney David Rocah also attacked the proposal: "Even if the license works as officials claim, every transaction done with the smart card will leave an electronic trial showing who did what and when. Computers will record each time the card is used to pay a toll, cash a check, make a purchase, check out a book, get insurance authorization to see your doctor, or any time you needed proof of identification. Unlike the databases that currently exist, all of these new databases will be able to be combined, because they will all share the same means of identifying the individual involved - your Social Security Number." Ah, Big Brother is alive and well, but was defeated this time. If you think it's a nightmare now when you lose your checkbook or credit card, imagine what it would be like if your entire history and ability to purchase anything was all tied to one number! If a thief got that number or it was lost in a computer system somewhere, what would you do then? Could you live for six months to a year (or longer) without buying any goods or services while the matter got corrected? Read on...

President Clinton signed Executive Order 13083 on May 14, 1998 while visiting the United Kingdom. Executive orders are enforceable, but not legislatively created regulations! First, well buried in the text, is a section that explains how the federal government will just have to take control if certain state activities seem to be out of hand (in the sole judgment of some federal government agency). The other key part is the statement that this order becomes effective in 90 days. Customarily executive orders of the president become effective in 30 days. It's especially significant when you look at the Notice of Proposed Rule Making that the Department of Transportation published, on June 17, 1998, three days after the executive order. Unless killed before October 14, 1998, the rules proposed by the Department of Transportation document will become effective October 1, 2000. Coupled with Clinton's declaration that legislation or regulation coming down from Washington is the new law of the land (state's rights anyone?), the DOT's rules will have more than just a power of suggestion! Fortunately, under great pressure from local and state legislators, governors, and common citizens, President Clinton suspended indefinitely his executive order in August of 1998.

The DOT published its proposed Driver's License / Social Security Number / National Identification Document guidelines which all states will be compelled to comply with. The Notice of Proposed Rule Making sets out the standard feature requirements for driver's license cards and other identification documents. States that do not comply will find that their citizens will not be allowed to participate in routine, life-essential functions after the imposed federal deadline of October 1, 2000. Nonconforming licenses will not be accepted for identification by any federal agency. Once implemented, no one in the U.S. will be able to engage in many basic, fundamental societal activities unless they carry with them at all times a conforming government-issued identification card. The requirement of Social Security Numbers on driver's licenses has since been rescinded, but because of the standardization requirements still in place, most states will be gathering the numbers anyway. Supposedly the regulations are to help control the influx of illegal aliens, but they are being promulgated against all citizens regardless of their status.

Citizens of the United States have a constitutional right to work for a living. See State v. Polakow's Realty Experts, Inc. 243 Ala. 441, 10 So.2d 461, 462 (1942). They also have the constitutional right to travel (in order to get to work or for whatever purpose). See Crandall v. Nevada, 73 U.S. (6 Wall.) 35, 49 (1868) We are all citizens of the United States, and as members of the same community must have the right to pass and repass through every part of it without interruption, as freely as in our own states. Also: Kent v. Dulles, 357 U.S. 116, 125, 78 S.Ct. 1113 (1958) The right to travel is a part of the 'liberty' of which the citizen cannot be deprived without the due process of law under the Fifth Amendment In Dunn v. Blumstein, 405 U.S. 330, 339, 92 S.Ct. 995 (1972) The court stated: Since the right to travel was a constitutionally protected right, 'any classification which serves to penalize the exercise of that right, unless shown to be necessary to promote a compelling governmental interest, is unconstitutional. In addition, the court stated: The right to travel is an 'unconditional personal right,' a right whose exercise may not be conditioned, Since having a Social Security Number is not a legal requirement for United States citizens and has nothing to do with the ability to drive a car, it is patently unreasonable to make the licensure for driving dependent on having a number which is not even legally required. The same argument applies to Canada.

Under the federal New Hires Database system and the related Employment Eligibility Confirmation System program, everyone will be required to possess an approved identification document in order to get a job and work in the United States. Also, as a condition of the new and upcoming healthcare-provider requirements, everyone will have to submit a conforming identification document in order to receive health care. Providers that don't cooperate will forfeit all federal compensation for their services (like Medicaid and Medicare). Of course other activities such as banking, purchasing insurance, writing a check, obtaining a passport, boarding a commercial airliner and innumerable other normal day to day activities will all likewise require the new IDs. The proponents of this measure are intent on establishing a universal, nationwide identification system and state-issued driver's licenses are the method they have chosen as the path of least resistance.

Under the Administrative Procedures Act federal agencies must announce their intention to promulgate new rules, (as they have now done in this case), and they must provide an opportunity for the general public to comment on their proposal. Will enough people know about this and express their opinion? The U.S. government has not been very responsive in the past about input from it's citizens, except through the Congress, which seems more interested in reelection campaign money than citizen's rights.

There are representatives in Congress who are fighting *for* your privacy rights. People like Ron Paul of Texas and Robert Barr of Georgia have introduced legislation which would defeat the National ID, or strengthen your control over personal information. But these efforts are usually watered down by the lobbyists from the information industry.

The Patient Privacy Rights Act, sponsored by Patrick Leahy of Vermont, would repeal the unique medical identifiers requirement of the Health Insurance Portability Law of 1996 (HIPAA). *That* bill was sponsored by former Sen. Nancy

Kassebaum (R-Kan.), and Sen. Edward Kennedy (D-Mass.) and directs the U.S. Department of Health and Human Services to develop a system to use personal identifying codes as part of a system for electronically transmitting health information to aid implementation of the health insurance portability law. These unique health identifiers would be codes, numbers, or other methods of uniquely identifying each patient. Doctors would be required to use the codes throughout that person's lifetime. Leahy had fought to delete the HIPAA mandate, which was not included in the Senate version of the bill, but it remained in the bill at the insistence of House leaders. Remember that at election time! There are ways of maintaining your privacy in your healthcare, but it is becoming increasingly difficult under current regulations. You might be able to pay with cash or use the services of organizations and practitioners who will not require Social Security Number's. See organizations in the Resource section for ones that can help you here.

In introducing the bill, Leahy continued, "Health care computerization not only is inevitable, it can be a useful tool to improve health care. But trusting our medical records to this rapidly developing technology will only be supported by the American people if they are assured that their medical privacy is protected." Privacy is not the only victim here. Without privacy protections, many will be discouraged from seeking help or taking advantage of the access we are working so hard to protect in this very same law.

Leahy also sponsored and introduced the Medical Information Privacy and Security Act, a comprehensive plan to safeguard the privacy of individuals' medical records. Other recent privacy related bills include:

- H.R. 220. Freedom and Privacy Restoration Act of 1999. Limits use of SSN, prohibits creation of gov't IDs. Sponsor: Ron Paul (R-TX).

- H.R. 354. Collections of Information Antipiracy Act. Creates new property rights for owners of databases of public information. Sponsor: Howard Coble (R-NC).
- H.R. 358. Patients' Bill of Rights Act of 1999. Requires health plans and insurers to protect confidentiality of medical records and allow patient access. Sponsor: John Dingell (D-MI).
- H.R. 367. Social Security On-line Privacy Protection Act of 1999. Limits disclosure of SSNs by interactive computer services. Sponsor: Rep Franks, Bob (R-NJ).
- H.R. 369. Children's Privacy Protection and Parental Empowerment Act of 1999. Prohibits the sale of personal information about children without their parents' consent. Sponsor: Bob Franks (R-NJ
- S. 6. Patients' Bill of Rights Act of 1999. Requires health plans and insurers to protect confidentiality of medical records and allow patient access. Sponsor: Tom Daschle (D-SD).
- S. 300. Patients' Bill of Rights Plus Act. Sets privacy protections. Prohibits genetic discrimination. Sponsor: Trent Lott (R-MS
- S. 326. Patients' Bill of Rights Act. Sets privacy protections. Prohibits genetic discrimination. Sponsor: James Jeffords (R-VT)

Further attention to the privacy problem has resulted partly as a result of some rather famous people and some legislators having been exposed on the Internet. When it hits home, it's a little more important. See the floor speech below given by Senator Diane Feinstein (D-CA) in support of S. 600, the Personal Information Privacy Act of 1997, cosponsored by Charles Grassley (R-IO).

> Mrs. FEINSTEIN: Mr. President, today, along with my distinguished colleague, Senator Charles Grassley, I am introducing the Personal Information Privacy Act of 1997. This legislation limits the accessibility and unauthorized

commercial use of Social Security Numbers, unlisted telephone numbers, and certain other types of sensitive personal information.

In November, the news media reported that companies were distributing Social Security Numbers along with other private information in their online personal locator or look-up services. In fact, I found that my own Social Security Number was accessible to users of the Internet. My staff retrieved it in less than 3 minutes. I have the printout in my files.

Some of the larger and more visible companies have now discontinued the practice of displaying Social Security Numbers directly on the computer screens of Internet users. Other enterprises have failed to modify their practices. One problem thwarting efforts to protect our citizens' privacy is that there are thousands of information providers on the Internet and elsewhere in the electronic arena, it is impossible to get a comprehensive picture of who is doing what, and where.

But one fact is clear, distributing Social Security Numbers on the Internet is only the tip of the iceberg. Too many firms profit from renting and selling Social Security Numbers, unlisted telephone numbers, and other forms of sensitive personal information. List compilers and list brokers use records of consumer purchases and other transactions, including medical purchases, along with financial, demographic, and other data to create increasingly detailed profiles of individuals.

The growth of interactive communications has generated an explosive growth in information about our interests, our activities, our illnesses, about the personal choices we make when we order products, inquire about services, participate in workshops, and visit sites on the Net.

A *Newsday* article titled 'Your Life as an Open Book' recently reported that an individual's call to a toll free number to learn the daily pollen count resulted in a disclosure to a pharmaceutical company that the caller was likely to have an interest in pollen remedies. It is true that knowledge about personal interests, circumstances, and activities can help companies tailor their products to individual needs and target their marketing efforts. But there need to be limitations.

Prior to the widespread use of computers, individual records were stored on paper in government file cabinets at scattered locations around the country. These records were difficult to obtain. Now, with networked computers, multiple sets of records can be merged or matched with one another, creating highly detailed portraits of our interests, our allergies, food preferences, musical tastes, levels of wealth, gender, ethnicity, homes, and neighborhoods. These records can be disseminated around the world in seconds.

What is the result? In addition to receiving floods of unwanted mail solicitations, people are losing control over their own identities. We don't know where this information is going, or how it is being used. We don't know how much is out there, and who is getting it. Our private lives are becoming commodities with tremendous value in the marketplace, yet we, the owners of the information, often do not derive the benefits. Information about us can be used to our detriment.

As an example, the widespread availability of Social Security Numbers and other personal information has led to an exponential growth in identity theft, whereby criminals are able to assume the identities of others to gain access to charge accounts and bank accounts, to obtain the personal records of others, and to steal Government benefits.

In 1992, Joe Gutierrez, a retired Air Force chief master sergeant in California became a victim of identity theft when a man used his Social Security Number to open 20 fraudulent accounts. To this day, Mr. Gutierrez has been hounded by creditors and their collection agencies. It is pure hell, he said in an interview with the *San Diego Union Tribune:* "They have called me a cheat, a deadbeat, a bum. They have questioned my character, my integrity, and my upbringing."

As an additional problem, the unauthorized distribution of personal information can lead to public safety concerns, including stalking of battered spouses, celebrities, and other citizens.

There are very few laws to protect personal privacy in the United States. The Privacy Act of 1974 is limited, and applies only to the use of personal information by the Government. With minor exceptions, the collection and use of personal information by the private sector is virtually unregulated. In other words, private companies have nearly unlimited authority to compile and sell information about individuals. As technology becomes more sophisticated, the ability to collect, synthesize and distribute personal information is growing exponentially.

The Personal Information Privacy Act of 1997 will help cut off the dissemination of Social Security Numbers, unlisted telephone numbers, and other personal information at the source.

First, the bill amends the Fair Credit Reporting Act to ensure the confidentiality of personal information in the credit headers accompanying credit reports. Credit headers contain personal identification information which serves to link individuals to their credit reports.

Currently, credit bureaus routinely sell and rent credit header information to mailing list brokers and marketing companies. This is not the use for which this information was intended. The bill we are introducing today would prevent credit bureaus from disseminating Social Security Numbers, unlisted telephone numbers, dates of birth, past addresses, and mothers' maiden names. This is important because this kind of information is subject to serious abuse: to open fraudulent charge accounts, to manipulate bank accounts, and to gain access to the personal records of others.

An exception is provided for information that citizens have chosen to list in their local phone directories. This means that phone numbers and addresses may be released if they already are available in phone directories.

As a second means of limiting the circulation of Social Security Numbers, the bill restricts the dissemination of Social Security Numbers by State departments of motor vehicles. Specifically, the bill amends certain exemptions to the Driver's Protection Act of 1994.

The legislation would prohibit State departments of motor vehicles from disseminating Social Security Numbers for bulk distribution for surveys, marketing, or solicitations. The bill requires uses of Social Security Numbers by State Departments of Motor Vehicles to be consistent with the uses authorized by the Social Security Act and by other statutes explicitly authorizing their use.

In addition to the above measures which will limit the accessibility of Social Security Numbers, the Personal Information Privacy Act of 1997 penalizes the unauthorized commercial use of Social Security Numbers.

Specifically, the bill amends the Social Security Act to prohibit the commercial use of a Social Security Number in the absence of the owner's written consent. Exceptions are provided for uses authorized by the Social Security Act, the Privacy Act of 1974, and other statutes specifically authorizing such use.

I believe this bill represents a major step in protecting the privacy of our citizens, and I urge my colleagues to support it. I ask unanimous consent that the text of the bill be included in the Record following our remarks.

It seems strange however, in light of Ms. Feinstein's concern for privacy as indicated by the above, that she also favors laws that require biometric identification, including fingerprints, retinal scans, DNA prints, and hand or facial digitized photos. These identifying records would be kept in national databanks, under whose control I wonder? Of course we can trust our government to protect our privacy here and to be able to avoid any mistakes with these records (right!). Certainly there would be no computer glitches or corrupted and lost files! The 6000 tapes the IRS "lost" are certainly an isolated case of mismanagement and there's no chance something like that could ever happen again! Likewise I'm sure no one in the government would be tempted to sell or otherwise benefit from these records (which could be used to control everything you do!) The intelligence agencies certainly wouldn't go on fishing expeditions through these records looking for "criminals"! Anyone who supports any controversial position would certainly be safe from government intimidation! After all, this *is* the land of the free! Isn't it?

Governmental files

If you have a Social Security Number, you're already in many governmental files (especially IRS files). If you don't have one, consider not getting one. The returns are dreadfully poor compared to what you can get investing for your retirement on your own and the benefits don't come close to outweighing the liabilities. Do not apply for a Tax ID number unless absolutely necessary and then mark boxes "for identification purposes only". Above your signature write: "All rights reserved to the course of common law without prejudice." This will help protect you in case you are challenged for any reason. We recommend that you avoid anything that is connected to a Social Security Number if at all possible. Granted, that can lead to inconveniences, but the benefits of anonymity are worth it. If you do have a number, you can attempt to find out what the government knows about you, though you may choose to abandon all connections between the number and yourself and avoid the hassle.

Keep in mind that governmental entities will use just about any method to track facts about your life and habits. These may not always rely on your Social Security Number, but it can be used to identify where you grew up (and maybe where you still have friends and relatives) and approximately how old you are. Information about you is becoming increasingly seen as a valuable commodity and state and local governments are using it to raise revenue, by selling it to information vendors. This information may or may not be accurate. Also, it is often easier for a stranger to get at it, than it is for you. A lot of the most pertinent details of your life are kept by local governmental agencies which are looking to raise money. When they computerize your public records, they may also make them available to scam artists or marketers looking to target certain populations (like rich widows, or families with certain diseases).

The following are all considered "public" information sources and are easily accessed by just about anyone:

Motor vehicle information, including personal data, traffic infractions and fines, and vehicle data (plus in some states, your Social Security Number)

Voting records - you may request that these be kept confidential if you have a strong case that revealing the information would pose a threat to your safety. You should never include your Social Security Number or phone on these records.

Birth, death, marriage and divorce certificates - usually kept in county court houses. These may also include Social Security Number's. If you're the best man for a friend, information about you may also be included on their records.

Property records - including descriptions of the property and former owners, plus the approximate value.

Court records - unless they involve a juvenile. Case files can be retrieved under the name of the plaintiff or the defendant.

The following are supposedly considered confidential:

Social Welfare records, including Medicare and Social Security benefits. Keep in mind however, that these are all available to the IRS.

Tax information - the IRS is supposed to keep this confidential, but regularly releases it to other governmental agencies.

School records - which may include information on social and emotional development, attitudes, psychological test scores, and even notes on private conversations with counselors or school social workers, in addition to grades, attendance, and activities. Federal law requires that if you are over the age of 18, you must authorize the release of any school records to others, including parents, but if the person is under 18, this same information can be released without consent to various local, state, and federal agencies. Persons over the age of 18 or parents have the right to examine all schools records and request that errors be corrected. Schools are also required to keep a log of all persons who have had access to student records.

Library records - most states make these records confidential (Hawaii, Ohio, Kentucky, and Mississippi do not). Privately funded libraries will have their own rules regarding privacy.

Criminal records - these are supposed to be confidential and only available to the accused, law enforcement agencies, attorneys, or agencies needing the information for licensing purposes. They may also be available to certain prospective employers like daycare providers for screening purposes. Many information management companies however are able to develop their own dossiers on people from information about arrests available publicly. They then make it available to employers seeking to do background checks.

Video store records - these are usually more private than just about anything else, though they too could be subpoenaed and investigators may be able to get information under false pretenses.

Sometimes an agency will restrict disclosure of information about you if you request it. You could indicate what uses of your private information are acceptable to you when you fill out a government form. It may not be honored, but it's worth the effort. You can also request from a government agency, the names and addresses of all agencies or persons who have requested information about you and the purpose of the inquiry. All states have "Open Records" laws the should allow you to see and correct your records. City and county records should also be available. Contact an attorney or one of the organizations listed in the resource section if an agency won't give you access to your records. You can learn about the privacy laws in your state at the following web site:

www.epic.org/privacy/consumer/states.html

Lexis-Nexis

One of the largest national databases is called P-TRAK on LEXIS-NEXIS. Information in the P-TRAK file is information readily available from publicly available information sources such as telephone directories and public records maintained by government agencies. The only information displayed is the individual's name, current address and up to two previous addresses and telephone numbers. In some cases, the individual's maiden or alias name may also appear as well as the month and year of birth. No other information is displayed. Only U.S. residents are included. Information contained in P-TRAK is derived from "header" information provided to LEXIS-NEXIS by a national consumer reporting agency. A sample record:

Name: Smith, John H.
Current Address: 123 Main Street, Omaha, NB 66666
Previous Addresses: 456 Oak Drive, Wilsonville, CA 94333 Birthdate: 2/1934
Telephone number: 111-222-4444
On file since: 4/12/1992

According to LEXIS-NEXIS, the company "... markets the P-TRAK file to the legal community for use by general legal practitioners, litigators and public attorneys, as well as law enforcement agencies and police departments." These professionals use the P-TRAK file to assist in locating litigants, witnesses, shareholders, debtors, heirs and beneficiaries. LEXIS-NEXIS is a business-to-business online service, not available to the general public.

The company has been sensitive to the privacy issue and has worked with the Federal Trade Commission to develop a set of "self-regulatory" principles and guidelines for the collection, handling, and dissemination of personal information. The FTC has praised LEXIS-NEXIS for its work in this area and in late 1997 concluded in its report to Congress that no new legislation is needed to regulate the individual reference services companies. This is very reassuring right? Its like saying that the wolf has declared that the sheep are very safe and need no further security because he has been assured by all of his wolf friends that they are safe. Other companies like LEXIS-NEXIS have pledged to act responsibly by only making information available for legitimate purposes "while taking into account the privacy concerns of the public." As a show of this concern, LEXIS-NEXIS discontinued the display of Social Security Numbers in the P-TRAK file in June 1996, 11 days after the product was introduced. You can acquire information by entering a Social Security Number by itself however. LEXIS-NEXIS says they will not display information about individuals designated as minors in its individual reference services products. You can request to have your name removed by sending your full name, complete address and telephone number by any of the following methods:

E-mail to: p-trak@prod.lexis-nexis.com
Mail to ATTN: P-TRAK, P.O. Box 933, Dayton, OH 45401
Internet: www.lexis-nexis.com/lncc/about/index.html
Fax to 1-800-732-7672

Name removal takes an average of 90 days from the receipt of the request and a letter of confirmation is sent upon removal. They claim that the information will be used solely to remove names from the P-TRAK database and they only accept removal requests from individuals. They do not support any third-party removal services.

According to LEXIS-NEXIS, they reload updated P-TRAK records and repeat the removal of names of those individuals who have previously requested removal. Even after removal, a person's name could reappear after a file update if the individual has recently applied for credit using a differently spelled name, new address, etc. To insure continued absence from the P-TRAK database, an individual would periodically have to repeat the removal process. I have no way of knowing if a request for removal would result in some kind of flag or special designation and suggest in general that a person use methods that allow them to disappear from public and privately held records silently, rather than to draw attention to themselves by contacting these database holders. In general, databases are increasingly linked and used to develop profiles or patterns of your life.

III. Strategies for Taking Back Control

It is my personal opinion that it's just too much trouble to try to completely eradicate your personal history, and therefore better to just develop a plan to stop adding more information, thereby gradually disappearing from public and private databases. There are many things you can do in both your personal and public life, in your financial affairs, and right in your own home.

12 Easy things you can do now

1. From now on, refuse to give out any personal data to strangers unless *absolutely* necessary (and then give out the very least necessary).
2. Stop entering contests and surveys and sending in product registration or warranty cards.
3. Browse the Internet and email anonymously.
4. Shred or burn financial documents you discard.
5. Don't talk about your finances or assets.
6. Instruct your children to not give out personal, identifying information, especially on the Internet.
7. Keep all sensitive documents in a secure place, but not in a bank safety deposit box (hide them or send to a private vault, hide a copy in a separate location).
8. Get your home address, phone number, Social Security Number, and driver's license number off your checks.

9. Don't say anything sensitive on cell phones, cordless phones, or any other communication device that uses the airwaves.
10. Be careful what toll-free numbers you call and never call them from a non-listed phone.
11. Get your name and phone number off your phone answering machine greeting.
12. Get an unpublished, unlisted number for all calls from family and friends. Put your other one on an answering machine and never answer it. NEVER write your unlisted, unpublished number down on any form or give it out to any business or government agency EVER!

The above will only get you started, but it's a good start. Doing nothing is making a decision to stay exposed to the dangers and threats to your credit, your assets, your identity, and your family. Below is a much more extensive list. You can pick and choose the items that pertain to you and which you can actually accomplish. Try to keep in mind all of the various aspects of your life I discussed earlier so you can come up with a comprehensive plan.

Protecting your identity

1. Keep a low profile. Don't boast about your privacy strategies or trust entities.
2. Don't give out personal information, especially to strangers.
3. Don't trust your banker, lawyer, accountant, or courier when it comes to your identity and personal privacy issues.
4. Don't discuss your financial affairs with anyone except those you trust the most.
5. You can purchase an international driver's permit not requiring a Social Security Number (and with a new identity name if you need complete privacy).

6. If you are a victim of a stalker or are in a situation where you need a complete identity change, you can change your name without any notification of anyone anywhere. You just start calling yourself something else. You can establish new ID from your old driver's license by merely renewing it and checking off name change. This won't stop a determined investigator or stalker who may have access to your number, but it will provide you with ID. You should check state regulations with regard to name changes on driver's licenses in your area. You can also establish a new identity with an International Driver's Permit and it is even possible to purchase a new birth certificate. Do not use these things to get any benefits from any government agency.
7. If you are in danger and need complete anonymity, purchase a book on changing identities, then follow the steps in it carefully. There are ways of acquiring a completely new persona, but you must do it right. See the resources section for books on identity.
8. Have utilities, phone bills, etc. in another person's name, a trust name, or a company name even if it means that you have to post funds in advance. This also applies to residential rental agreements.
9. In general, don't patronize businesses that ask for identifying information. This includes video stores and "club" stores (unless you provide them with a completely phony name and then *never* use a credit or debit card for purchases, only cash).
10. If you will be keeping your licenses, including driver's license and professional licenses, be sure to at least have the addresses changed to reflect a private mail drop or secretarial service address.

What to do at home

1. Keep personal data in a secure location. This includes Social Security cards, credit cards, licenses, birth certificates, old driver's licenses, documents with credit card

numbers, PIN numbers, bank account numbers, utility bills, telephone calling cards, marriage certificates, and passports. The preceding also applies to data on your spouse and children.

2. Use a private post office box or secretarial service for all mail.
3. If you choose to continue to use credit and enslave yourself to debt, order a copy of your credit report yearly and look for irregularities such as new accounts, address changes, and unusual activity.
4. Regularly review all monthly statements from all credit cards, banks, and utility companies (for that matter, any bill you receive).
5. Check for timely receipt of any newly ordered credit cards.
6. Don't print your Social Security Number or your phone number on your checks. If someone asks for a phone number say it is unlisted and private. If they won't take a check without a phone number, you can give a phony one or do business elsewhere. (Don't write bad checks.)
7. Don't ever give out any personal information when using a cordless or cell phone regardless of who you are talking to (assume others are listening).
8. Don't ever give out personal information to bank, credit card, or other financial institution "employees" who call you. There is no legitimate reason for them to get information this way. Get the name and number of the institution and then call back asking for the supervisor.
9. Never write down your PIN numbers unless you have a secret and secure place to put them. Remember to change them regularly.
10. Use an answering machine, caller ID and call block, or a voice mail service to screen calls. Don't accept calls from people who block their calls from caller ID.
11. Get a non-listed, non-published phone number and be very selective about who gets the number.
12. Use a door slot, secure locking mail box, or mail drop for all mail.

13. Don't fill out a forwarding address form at the post office. Notify all correspondents yourself.
14. Use a cross-shredder or burn (then stir ashes) all identifying documents from all financial transactions except for those you keep in a safe place (NOT a safety deposit box at a bank - see resources for private vaults). Include in this list items like credit card envelopes, match books, notes and scribbles, and anything else that shows information about what you do or who you are.
15. Don't get behind on credit card or mortgage payments.
16. Don't dial 800 numbers from a secure phone. You will reveal your number to whoever you call.
17. Don't get into disputes with landlords or tenants.
18. Remember that building permits are public record. Thousands of small time home remodelers and do-it-yourselfers never get permits and never get asked. If you do something major to your house though, you may have trouble when trying to sell it as the banks often want to see all the permits.
19. Don't get checks delivered to your home unless you have a locked mail box. Pick them up at the bank. Consider not having a checking account at a domestic bank.
20. Be careful about your trash. Put incriminating garbage in someone else's can (divorce investigators will often use "high" alcohol use - whatever that is, as an excuse in court cases for denying child custody).
21. Request to be omitted from reverse/city directories
22. Don't hire young baby sitters who live near your house. Find one that doesn't know your family and then pay in cash. Look up nannies in the phone book and use a service that does background checks.
23. Instruct magazines and organizations to which you belong to not share your address with direct marketers or anyone else. If they won't cooperate, don't do business with them.
24. If your name is on your gas meter, you might want to obliterate it.
25. Don't have garage sales at your house if a permit is required.

26. Don't give out credit card numbers over the phone unless you have initiated the call and are sure of the company. Consider leaving the credit card game and closing all your accounts.
27. Remember that baby monitors are easy to listen in on.
28. Don't use return addresses (or use your private P.O. box and a zip code if you do).
29. Don't announce your phone number or name on your outgoing answering machine message.
30. Don't put your name on the outside of your apartment mail box, put it on the inside for use only by the letter carrier.
31. You could have a phone line installed at a nearby friend's house and have it forwarded to your private secure phone in your house (which is also listed in someone else's name). Phone companies will usually allow you to give only a driver's license number or some other number, like a passport (which you can get without a Social Security Number if you do so for religious purposes), for identification. You could then restrict all calls on your secure line to only those originating from your friend's forwarded number. Be careful about who you give out that number to, and never give out your secure number.
32. Ask to have a password put on your phone, utility, and credit accounts.
33. Use your private P.O. box as the address on your checks.
34. Don't place classified ads displaying your secure phone number. Use a voice mail number or one that is a regular listed number.

At school

Schools will ask for a Social Security Number, but you are not required to provide one as they are purely voluntary and you can merely say so. Then you just provide them with an identification number you make up. You must be careful with forms that your children bring home, or make out at school. These may be very intrusive and be completely inappropriate in terms of the service being offered. Be aware also that some teachers are giving their students projects or papers to write that ask for very personal and private information about home life. You should instruct your children that no one at school has a right to delve into your personal affairs. School districts and state agencies have been known to go on fishing expeditions looking for signs of "child abuse", whatever they deem that to be. Here again, some egomaniac bureaucrat is deciding your moral code and you don't have to permit it. For college students:

1. Refuse to provide your Social Security Number or Social Insurance Number as a student ID. Instead make up a number and tell them you are doing so to protect your privacy. Schools usually use that ID number on everything, including posting of grades outside instructors' offices. Don't provide your Social Security Number for *anything* connected with any school.
2. Use a private mail drop instead of the one at the college.
3. Be absent on school picture day if visual identity is ultra sensitive for you or you are being stalked.
4. Use a private mail box when you register, not your physical home address.
5. Leave the phone number blank on your registration.

In general

1. Don't enter contests or sweepstakes.
2. Don't participate in any surveys whether written or on the phone (you could answer only how many live in your house on the census and claim your 5th amendment rights for the rest of the questions).
3. Don't get parking or traffic tickets. Obey the laws, it's not that difficult.
4. Return library books on time.
5. Write to get off junk mail lists and <u>on</u> no soliciting phone calls lists.

6. Don't return warranty cards or registration cards. Don't register your software electronically. Microsoft may search your entire hard disk for their products when you do so, recording every piece of software you have and then comparing it with registration and tech support data.
7. If you must, try to divorce amicably. If that's not possible, be sure to have your assets private and be prepared to make some major adjustments in your business affairs.
8. Don't use personalized (vanity) license plates.
9. Don't run for political office. Instead, support candidates and positions you like.
10. Contribute to charities and political campaigns with a money order and don't include your name or address.
11. Don't write letters to the editor unless you use your alias name and private mail box. Newspapers are scanned for names and they always want your name, address, and phone when you write letters to the editor.
12. Don't use "preferred customer" cards.
35. Don't go to court to change your name, just call yourself whatever you wish.
36. Don't contribute to political campaigns, except anonymously.
37. Put all of your important assets into pure common law trusts or other similar off-shore protected entities.
38. Avoid getting a concealed weapon's permit or registering a gun. If you think you need one, there are gun shows and auctions where you can buy one from collectors. Don't buy one from a gun shop.
39. Don't broadcast your CB radio call sign.
40. Don't get listed in any *Who's Who* book.
41. If you feel that you must register your pet, use a name that does not have a Social Security Number attached to it (better yet, consider not registering your pet).
42. Don't register your pattern, wedding gift preferences, or baby gift ideas at the department store.
43. Don't put identifying symbols or stickers on your car including Student of the Month, or "I'm proud to be ..." stickers).

44. Don't drop business cards in the "Free Lunch" bowl
45. Have documents notarized (if you must) in another state or county.
46. Use mail drop (private P.O. box) for driver's license and car registration.
47. Don't put your ham radio call sign on your license plates.
48. Don't use personal property as collateral to borrow money.
49. Consider the implications and benefits of applying for citizenship elsewhere.
50. Consider not printing an obituary for deceased loved ones.
51. Never reveal your PIN numbers to anyone for any reason.
52. Don't ignore the calls of bill collectors or government agencies. Deal with the issue so you don't become a red flag.
53. Tell family members NOT to reveal personal information in general, but especially to strangers.
54. Don't sign guest registers at museums, national parks, tourist locations/guest houses, etc.
55. Don't give out your Social Security or Social Insurance Number. If you want to be in the system, limit it to the absolutely bare minimum. Consider alternatives to bank accounts, licenses, etc. that might require it.
56. Settle or win all lawsuits quickly to eliminate outstanding judgments.
57. Don't use your spouse's maiden name to try to disguise a trust or other entity's identity or password. Investigators have been on to this trick for a long time. Don't use it when opening a bank account either. Also, don't use your children's names or any name that has anything to do with you or your family for any trust or other financial entity you want to keep private.
58. Don't get behind on alimony/child support payments. You'll be a special target if you do so and then leave the state. Recent federal laws have made this a big time crime.
59. Don't file fictitious name statements.
60. Read every contract or application and look for waivers of your right to privacy. This includes medical forms. You

might be able to specify that your current visit or condition is not to be generally disclosed.

61. Don't rent videos from stores that require personal information, use cash deposits.
62. Use the short version of your name when you can (Bill Jones, not William B. Jones Jr.)
63. Always sign your name in upper and lower case letters, NEVER in all upper case. The correct spelling of John William Jones is John-Williams: Jones with the hyphen and colon.
64. Don't permanently stick company, school or apartment complex parking stickers on you car.
65. Don't be a best man or maid of honor unless you scribble your name and address.
66. Don't sue anyone - avoid *being* sued.
67. Consider not voting and not registering to vote. You can achieve more by being an activist anyway. If you feel that you must register to vote, be creative with your occupation, and never list a phone number. While voting is still an important method of voicing your opinion, you put yourself at risk if you are the victim of a stalker and you may have to forgo this right. You may wish to vote in local elections, but keep in mind that national ones are mere polls anyway, with leaders chosen by others behind the scenes.
68. Get married overseas or by a person who doesn't require identifying numbers or government registration (see resource list).
69. Don't get a radio license, or any other licenses if you can possibly avoid them and not get in trouble.
70. Don't file for bankruptcy if you can avoid it. Sometimes this is an important method of dealing with creditors however and also part of a strategy for removing yourself from the "system."
71. Consider not using your Social Security or Social Insurance Number again for anything. Start disassociating yourself from everything that has anything to do with it. Be prepared

with an alternative 9 digit number, but be sure you let people know it's not an SSN, it's your alternative ID number.

72. Be aware of video and audio recording devices in public places and in all places of business, including hotels, rented apartments, houses, and offices. Consider at least doing a cursory check for these devices.
73. Be wise in how you deal with the income tax issue. If you decide you aren't liable for any particular tax, be sure to follow instructions carefully. Don't mix strategies. Remember, you want to avoid ending up in U.S. Tax Court or have to fight Revenue Canada. Don't count on winning there unless you are well prepared.

Computers

Your computer, whether at home or at the office probably contains a great deal of information about you. Access to your computer may be accidental or intentional. You should maintain the same high level of security on all computers that contain personal information. To gain an understanding of the type of information that can be captured from your computer over the Internet, you can visit the Center for Democracy and Technology's web site at www.cdt.org. There are two main threats to your privacy and to the data on your computer: 1) Information stolen or copied when transmitted over a modem, especially the Internet. 2) Actual physical theft of hardware or files copied to floppy disks. The following tips apply anywhere regardless of your general usage or circumstances:

1. Keep your computer in a locked room.
2. Never leave a portable or laptop computer unattended especially in an airport.
3. Use a keyboard or power-supply locking device.
4. Use a locking base or steel cable to prevent moving the computer.
5. Use a key-lock device to prevent use of the floppy drive.

6. Use software password utilities or encryption programs to block others from accessing the contents of your files.
7. Keep backups of important files or even the entire hard drive in a secure place. A tape backup is the cheapest and easiest to use.
8. Purge "deleted" files frequently (empty the recycle bin) and consider using special utility programs that wipe the contents of deleted files by replacing them with random characters.
9. Remember that data on formatted floppy or hard disks can be "recovered" by experts.
10. Be very careful about programs given to you by anyone. Viruses, trojan horse programs, and other software might damage your files or provide an entry way into your computer from others over the Internet.
11. Always keep your virus checking program up to date and use one that provides continuous checking of your computer's activity.
12. If you definitely have sensitive data on your computer, you may want to use software utilities that track all activity. Then be sure to review the logs frequently.
13. Avoid the Intel PIII chip that has a built-in identifier. You can buy the Intel PII or CPU's from AMD or Cyrix and get excellent performance without the exposure.
14. Imagine everything you type as email (unless encrypted) being put on a highway billboard.

Internet browsers, and computer files

In June of 1998, the Federal Trade Commission said a review of more than 1,400 Web sites showed that roughly 85 percent fail to tell visitors how personal data they collect would be used. Email is just plain not secure unless it's encrypted. For the most part, neither is anything else you do on the Internet unless you take precautions. Many sites offer encrypted transactions for forms submittals and credit card purchases. Such sites typically have URLs starting with https:// instead of http:// and are considered quite secure, certainly enough for credit card transactions. You can look for some indication of a secure site by looking for a key or broken key icon or a padlock that is either closed or open. It should not surprise you that the U.S. government has attempted to diminish the use of this technology so that the FBI or other agencies can read anything (always under the guise of a threat to national security, their catchall phrase for anything that they want to be able to examine). Browsers therefore generally have one of two levels of security:

1. International security - the only level allowed for export outside of North America. It uses codes and encryption that can be cracked by organized criminals and sophisticated amateurs. It is limited to 56 bit encryption. A recent international compact called the Wassenaar Arrangement was signed in early 1999 by 33 industrialized countries agreeing to restrict export and impose controls on data-scrambling technologies, including mass-marketed software like PGP. The agreement applies to products using 56 bit keys or greater. You can see it at the following web site: www.wassenaar.org. The intent appears to be to squash proliferation of high level encryption programs in the name of arms control. Recently this agreement was bypassed by a loosening of cryptographic regulations by the U.S., allowing all levels to be used. Exceptions were made to disallow sales to countries the U.S. considers to be "rogue" or supporting terrorism, like Iraq and Cuba.

2. U.S. security - available only for the U.S. and Canada. This level uses encryption believed to be unbreakable except by very large governments with unlimited resources (such as the U.S. government).

Your computer probably uses the weaker security, especially if your browser came bundled with the computer or you downloaded it off the Internet. You should absolutely check out especially the SSL level of your browser. Most people are probably using the weaker 40 bit level that comes standard. You can check the level of your browser at www.e-gold.com/unsecure/aboutssl.html. You can also check the general level of protection your computer has at www.grc.com. The government has been trying to convince us that the DES standard of 56 keys is sufficient, but recently an independent nonprofit foundation cracked a DES code in less than 3 days using off-the-shelf hardware costing less than $250,000. Organized crime has much more sophisticated equipment available to them, as do government intelligence agencies. To protect yourself you'll need to use anonymous browsing and email such as that provided by www.anonymizer.com/. This company disguises your identity so that it cannot be traced back to your Internet address. It even has some new services that allow you to use the company as an Internet service provider and even *they* won't know who you are because all you do is select a name and password, then send them a monthly fee (in cash or money order).

Additionally, you may want to use a good encryption program for any sensitive email. PGP uses the much stronger 1024 bit encryption, but is weakened by the public key component. If you don't publish your public key you'll be fine and 1024 bit encryption is even too strong for the government (unless you are on their most wanted list). Send it to important people on a disk via courier, or physically hand it to them. Alternately, you can encrypt a file and use the "Conventional encryption" feature, which will then let you set a password you can give to the recipient. When they type in the password, the file is automatically decrypted. This works great for sending encrypted files as attachments in email. If you want to communicate to people outside the US, consider the international version, or buy an encryption program from another country. Look up "blowfish" on the Internet and you'll find scores of programs that use this excellent encryption algorithm and are from countries not subject to the outrageous US laws.

Another potential weak spot in your Internet usage is the use of plug-ins, helper programs, ActiveX Controls, and mini-programs called RPC's (Remote Procedure Calls). These programs allow for all kinds of fancy displays or effects like sound and animation. They give your browser extra capabilities that aren't built in already. One major security hole that Microsoft knows exists, but they refuse to correct is ActiveX Controls. This program code actually allows anything to happen to your computer or hard drive, including copying all of your files to a remote location and then formatting your drive. An ActiveX Control could also contain a virus which will not be caught by your anti-virus software before it starts its dirty work. It starts to function automatically when you access a web page unless you have disallowed it in the preferences section of security settings. ActiveX Controls can be written for *any* purpose whatsoever and are a major part of the Microsoft operating system, so are not only very powerful, but can be very dangerous. You can read all about ActiveX controls at the following site: www.halcyon.com/ActiveX/Exploder/FAQ.htm (written by an expert web consultant who has communicated his concerns to Microsoft).

Caches and histories

A cache is a file that records your activity. It may be left in memory or on your hard disk. Browsers record 3 things whenever you visit a web site:

1. The page itself in your cache
2. The URL of the page in your history
3. The URL's *you typed in* at the URL box (drop down list)

You probably have both a memory and hard disk cache on your computer depending on whether it's a MAC or PC and on the operating system.

AOL

You should check your www/internet properties. Go to the navigation tab and clear history. You can also set history to zero. Under the security tab, don't allow active-X controls. Set safety level to highest. Under advanced, set warn on for everything. Under temporary Internet files, look in the settings and empty the folders, then set it for only 1% of the hard disk space. Under personal filing cabinet on the preferences screen, keep the size of the file low. Check the "download" folder in the AOL directory (folder) for files you may want to delete. Better yet, don't use AOL at all! Poor security, poor service, and limited capabilities make this my least favorite Internet service provider.

Microsoft's Internet Explorer

Microsoft has spent a great deal of time and energy to incorporate browser technology into all of its products since it "got the Internet religion" back in 1997. In order to protect yourself from threats to your files, you should set the security preferences at the highest level and disallow Active-X controls. I also recommend disallowing cookies. The methods for doing this depends on the version and hardware that you are using. Be sure to also clear history, disk and memory caches frequently. An easier way to do all of this is to buy a program that can be set to do it for you. Jetico at www.jetico.com makes a variety of programs to accomplish this. There are many other products on the market today too, like Zorosoft's Privacy Restored! (www.zorosoft.com), and they are not expensive, so you have no excuse. Using a program like this makes sure that you haven't forgotten anything.

Netscape

Clearing the cache:

While in Netscape select Options|Network Preferences or Edit|Preferences|Advanced. In the dialog box, click the Cache tab. Now click on both the [Clear Memory Cache Now] and [Clear Disk Cache Now] buttons. Then click on [OK].

Alternately you can delete all files in your \Netscape\Cache directory.

Clearing the history:
Select Options|Network Preferences|Appearance or Edit|Preferences Navigator. Now click on the [Expire Now] or the [Clear History] button. Then click on [OK]. Alternately you can delete netscape.hst in your \Netscape directory. Check out the following sites for programs that clear the history for you:

www.zorosoft.com
www.nsclean.com
www.2020tech.com/maildrop/privacy.html

The cleaning programs also take care of cookies and other potential incriminating files left by Internet use. The latest versions of Netscape Navigator and Internet Explorer allow you to disable cookies or have a warning whenever they occur, but you can also purchase specific programs to take care of this little problem. See Pretty Good Privacy's Cookie Cutter, at www.pgp.com, and Kevin McAleavey's program at www.wizvax.net/kevinmca. Nsclean and IEClean also delete cookies and a whole lot more at the click of a button.

Email

Your email name and address is pretty much public property. Whether it should be or not, you should consider it to be so in actuality. Professional spammers (people or companies that distribute email to thousands of addresses at once) use a variety of methods to get your name and address.

- They buy or rent it from your Internet service provider.
- They get it from the "from:" section of your email header.
- They get it from you when you include it in your signature.

- Your children give it to them when they play games or visit sites offering free gifts.
- They get it from you when you respond to email offers.
- They put you <u>on</u> their list when you ask to be removed.
- They check addresses of people who post or respond to usenet sites.
- They get if from participants of chat rooms.
- They get it from your biographical profile you give to your Internet service provider (especially AOL).
- They captured it while you were listing yourself in "people-finder" directories (these are often monitored for new data).
- You gave it to them when you participated in an email chain letter.
- You gave it to them when you entered an online contest, sweepstakes, game, poll, or survey.
- They captured it when you registered with a web site, email mailing list, publication, announcement service, reminder service, or "software updating service".
- They captured it when you purchased something online or filled out a product registration card.
- You provided it in your web site "mailto" link and their robots picked it up.

Email is a terrific new invention, but it is a privacy nightmare unless encrypted. Keep in mind also that all your email goes through many other computers before reaching it's destination. Bits and pieces of it are left and then gathered up all over the country. It works very well, but unencrypted, it is about as secure as yelling down the street. Even deleted email is only deleted on *your* computer unless you have it set for deletion from the server also. (Even then it may be on backups at your service provider) You should always empty your trash after deleting email messages. Remember however, that the email may have been intercepted before it got to you and read by anyone in Cyberspace. Encrypting email with a good encryption program is the only way to protect yourself. Search for encryption with any of the search engines. One particular site that has a wide variety of products available using the Blowfish algorithm is www.counterpane.com/products.html. I always recommend using at least 256 bit encryption.

Email creates difficulty for anonymity since the sender of a message can be traced back through its paths. Email anonymity may be very important if you are a whistle blower, writer of controversial material or even just need the ability to write to someone with no forwarding address. Remailers conceal the source by sending it through an anonymous *new* source. See the following sites for information about people who run remailers:

www.gilc.org/speech/anonymous/remailer.html
www.ozemail.com.au/~geoffk/anon/anon.html
www.zeroknowledge.com

If your browser uses Java, you'll have to follow the instructions you find on the latter page for turning some of Java's security features off. Some remailers are more complicated and require special software. Others may be run as government entrapment devices, so beware, and consider encryption for added security. You can get information about these services at:

http://infotrek.simplenet.com/anonymous.html
www.stack.nl/~galactus/remailers/index.html
www.anonymizer.com

By using a remailer, your actual email address, normally found in the message header, is concealed. The anonymizer site uses mixmaster technology to randomize email messages before using a remailer. You can also use this site to surf the web anonymously, as a service provider, or even as an anonymous web site publisher. They also have many excellent links to other privacy resources. One very good remailer was created as a joint project of the George Mason Society and the Global Internet Liberty Campaign, available at:

www.gilc.org/speech/anonymous/remailer.html. You might also want to visit the following sites for info on remailers and mixmasters:

> www.stack.nl/~galactus/remailers/index-mix.html
> www.jpunix.com/

Be warned that the U.S. government is currently running remailer sting operations and you will not know if the one you use is being monitored. For that reason, we recommend that you also encrypt any sensitive files you attach to email messages and never say anything sensitive in the subject line or message text. Use PGP freeware to encrypt the attached file using the "Conventional" feature and then give the file a password which you must relay to the recipient via phone, in person, or another way (not through email).

You can also get an email account at www.dejanews.com and use their web site to post messages to newsgroups anonymously. In general, you should try to avoid putting anything sensitive in the subject area. If you wish, put something there that is totally innocuous and has nothing to do with anything important, like "a new recipe". You should also avoid anything of any importance in the first 2 lines of your message, since these, along with the subject are the things that are intercepted the most to look for "activity" by snoops.

A new industry has developed with the emergence of the Internet called email address compilers. One large such company is called Bigfoot Directory. They claim to have over 11 million email addresses worldwide and are reportedly adding a million new addresses every month. They also have phone numbers, addresses, fax numbers and former email addresses, all in six languages. They sell these lists to most anyone who will pay, but have a "privacy list" of names for people who don't want unsolicited email. Such mail, called spam is very widespread and not generally illegal, though it is very unpopular and spammers are often the recipients of extremely negative responses. A recently passed new law in the state of

Washington makes illegal the concealment of header information in any email going to a Washington recipient. This law was subsequently ruled unconstitutional in court. Spammers are very good at concealing the origin of their messages and are quite difficult to track down, though it can be done. The government is grappling with this issue now, but don't look for any help soon as the right of free-speech is a major component. At the present time it's probably best just to use an email program that allows you to filter messages and send spam directly to the trash. Otherwise, always request that your name *not* be added to email lists if that option is available. You can contact Bigfoot at their web site www.bigfoot.com. Other directories to contact are:

www.switchboard.com
www.four11.com
www.whowhere.com
www.infospace.com

You can also use various email aliases for different purposes and visit the following sites for help in fighting spam:

www.mcs.com/~jcr/junkemail.html
www.coyotecom/jac/stopjunk.html

Cookies

These are bits of information contained in files left on your computer when you visit a web site. They contain information about where you went in the site, how often you visit, what you clicked on and other such things as your log-in name and site password, your billing address and credit card number, and a "user profile" which gives the web site information about your preferences and needs. Browsers are *supposed* to enforce rules for the use of cookies including limiting their file size to 4k bytes, having an expiration date, and only allowing access by the site that sent them. You should set cookies off or set your browser to always warn of cookies. Look in Edit, Tools, Options, or Preferences in your browser. You might also have to click on a protocols tab. You should be able to do everything you want to do *without* accepting cookies. If you want to leave them on, use the search facility on your computer to periodically delete any files on your computer with the following name format: cookies*.* You could write a batch file to do this automatically every time you start or terminate a Web session if you feel that you want to allow cookies because it's too much trouble to always refuse them. The anonymizer folks disable cookies for you (as well as java script) so you don't have to worry. See www.anonymizer.com/ for all of their services. You can also check the "anonymous" section in Andre Bacard's web site at www.well.com/user/abacard/index.html.

One nice thing about using Netscape is that it puts all the cookie information into one file, as opposed to Microsoft's Internet Explorer, which allows many cookie files. You can use Notepad to erase everything in the Netscape cookie file (cookies.txt) and then save it, followed by setting it to read only in preferences. You an then set Netscape to accept all cookies knowing that the file won't be changed.

Swap files

These are files used to make a computer run more programs than can be held in available memory. Data is simply written to disk and back again to memory as needed. The problem is that anything can be written to disk in a swap file and later read by someone without your best interests at heart. Deleting a swap file can have serious consequences and is different for each operating system. We recommend a file wiping utility like PGP, Norton, or BCWipe. These programs take care of securely wiping deleted files AND clean your swap file.

Deleted files

Files are not really deleted when you "delete" them, but are merely "marked" for deletion and the space made available for overwriting. These can be overwritten or "wiped" by a utility designed for this purpose. See section above on swap files. When you empty your recycle bin in Windows 95, the files should not be available, but some utilities could actually recover them if someone wanted to bad enough and the files weren't overwritten by other data. You will also want to close all applications and delete files in your Windows\temp directory (if you're using Win95 or 3.x). A good web site for information on getting rid of files is: www.stack.nl/~galactus/remailers/index-wipe.html. Another one sells a program called Shredder that purports to make deleted files unrecoverable. Their web site is at: www.stratfor.com/. There are many good products out there but Jetico (www.jetico.com) makes a good encryption program and file wiper. It's file wipe program BCWipe also takes care of slacks space which is the space left over when a file is deleted and bits and pieces of it are left in parts of the cluster it occupied. That cluster may be re-used by another file, but the parts of the cluster not used by the new file will contain data connected with the deleted file and this data can later be read by sophisticated utility programs used by investigators or data recovery experts.

Log files

These files also contain a record of your activity. They are often used in news readers. You should look for a file with a name like newsrc or possibly a file with the word "news" in the name and "rc" for an extension. Look in directories that might contain the word news or host or cache. You can edit these files with a text editor deleting all references to Internet or newsreader locations you'd like to eliminate. Make sure the file stays in text form when you save. For instance, news readers need the names of news groups and currently there are over 40,000. When you open up your news reader or the one built into your browser, the program needs the names of all the groups. Unless you want to download a new listing every time, a very time consuming task, you'll want to use your old listing. The trouble is, that listing may also identify all of the places that you visited, ie. the names of the news groups that you listed out messages on. These groups may be perfectly OK to *you*, but offensive to someone else who has a different belief system from you. Sure its your business, but why open yourself up for problems. Remember that posting a message always logs your presence and identity (unless you use an anonymous ID or anonymizer program).

One thing you can do is to download the latest group listing and then save a copy of it with a new name like newsrc.sav. Then go ahead and browse the newsgroups you wish (being aware of potential identifying activities and sting operations), but deleting the newsrc file when done and finally copying the newsrc.sav file to newsrc without an extension (or whatever its name is supposed to be for your reader). This way you always have a copy of the group listing file without any indication of your visits.

If you don't know the name of the file used to contain group listings and you use Windows 95, look for the directory where the newsreader is located (look for "news" or some variation), open up your news reader and go to some innocuous group like alt.ads, then click on a couple of messages, and finally close it and go to your file manager. Sort by date (click on the date tab). Note the file that has just changed. You can then open it up with Word Pad and check to see if it's the right file. It should contain a listing of groups and the one you visited should have a couple of extra numbers or codes at the end of the listing.

Profiles and passwords

AOL was caught giving information about a gay sailor to the Navy in June of 1998, in violation of its own term of service agreement. A Navy investigator posing as a civilian, contacted

AOL's customer service department and got information that was listed in his profile. In January of 1998, U.S. District Court Judge Stanley Sporkin ruled that the investigation was illegal under the Electronic Communications Privacy Act, and the government could not use the material against the sailor. He sued and was awarded damages from both AOL and the Navy. AOL has said that they will strengthen their training procedures so that sensitive information is not given out, but you need to protect yourself and not count on any Internet service provider to protect your identity or personal information. For instance, you may feel that your ISP violated your agreement, but then would you sue in federal court for breach of contract? Federal courts may not have jurisdiction. If you sued in a state court, you might lose on the basis of interpretation as each state has it's own idea of privacy, or it may not accept jurisdiction either. Also, some agreements require subscribers to submit to private arbitration, which could prevent a court solution altogether. You might want to check the term of service agreement you signed with your provider. It may not prevent them from giving out personal information about you. The Electronic Communications Privacy Act has loopholes in it that allow private citizens access to information on the Internet even though government agencies are supposed to be required to have a warrant, a court order, or the consent of the subscriber. Keep in mind also that bulletin boards and chat-room email are often permanently archived and could later be used against you. The best course of action is to cover yourself and not count on the government or the industry to protect your privacy or your rights.

It has been reported that AOL also does not protect its member's passwords adequately. Members have been able to call their billing department and, giving only name and home address, change the password with no problem at all. Supposedly AOL is strengthening this area too, but you should not assume that they have done so. AOL's CEO, Steve Case reported in January, 1998 that it's reps handled over a million calls per week. There have been many stories about AOL accounts being compromised and Mr. Case has personally admitted that they had divulged a subscriber's real-life name on various occasions. He still states however "AOL's commitment to protecting the privacy of our members is stronger than ever." Now that's reassuring!

Children on the Internet

There are many sites on the Internet that encourage children to give out sensitive and personal information. Kids are often lured into these sites by games or promises of free gifts or prizes. Once there, the site's real purpose is to gather information about their families and then sell it to marketers. The Federal Trade Commission found in a study concluded in June of 1998 that 89 percent of the 212 child-oriented Web sites it surveyed collected personal data from kids. Of those, only 54 percent disclosed their practices and less than ten percent sought parental approval. In response, the FTC has recommended legislation to control gathering of personal information on child oriented sites. Again, don't wait for the government to protect you! You should tell your kids to *never* give out any personal information over the Internet, just as they wouldn't give it out to a stranger on the street! After you tell them, check up, by watching them periodically. Look closely at the sites they visit, just like you'd check out movies or television programs they are exposed to. More and more sites are refusing to allow children under 13 to have email accounts and/or are requiring proof of adult permission. Nevertheless, you need to supervise your children.

Electronic anonymity and the internet

An old physics law says that for every action there is an opposite and equal reaction. That seems to be the case in the electronics world too. For every way that someone invents to spy on you, there's probably a way to defeat it. One effective form of completely anonymous network communication, called Onion Routing, was developed by Navy researchers David Goldschlag and Paul Syverson. Instead of connecting your machine directly to another machine, thus leaving an electronic footpath to your identity, they would have you connect to an Onion Router. The Onion Router opens an anonymous connection through, say, five other Onion Routers, that ultimately lead to the intended destination. When your data arrives at the first Onion Router it gets encrypted five times, once for each router. The data is then sent along through subsequent Onion Routers getting decrypted along the way, and arriving on the other end as plain text. Someone responding to you would have to go through the same process, but would have no way to trace you because each Onion Router can only identify the next one down the line, making it impossible for someone to find the complete path of your original data. Plus, when the connection is broken, the Onion Routers dump any information related to your connection. You don't have to trust the network to protect your anonymity, explains Syverson. No network router has all the information. There are multiple layers of security with nothing in the middle, hence the onion metaphor. And it can be used for anything from email to web surfing. All that encrypting and routing does take its toll in the form of speed. The routing itself isn't any slower than using a proxy server such as anonymizer.com (which is now offering higher-speed anonymous browsing for $15 per quarter along with its free service), but the system overall is slower because of the encryption process taking place at each router - a small tradeoff, says Goldschlag, in exchange for increased privacy.

The trouble with anonymous remailers is that you're essentially entrusting someone else with your data. "We want to move the trust as close to the user as possible," says Syverson. Still, remailers aren't at all bad if you're just looking to send a piece of anonymous email or post to Usenet. Anonymous remailers basically take your message, strip away the header data that contains your name and location and send it on to the recipient. But the Church of Scientology recently proved that with enough legal might, even the staunchest privacy advocates could be forced to hand over the log files from their anonymous servers. In response, a group of cypherpunks invented a new type of remailer called a "Mixmaster." Unlike traditional remailers, mixmasters encode the message on your desktop and then lets you send it through a series of anonymous remailers. For a full list of remailers and mixmasters, consult the remailers directories at either Rutgers or U.C. Berkeley. If you're looking for a simpler but slightly less secure privacy tool for everyday browsing, try Intermute. This application not only blocks advertising banners, thus speeding downloads, it also disguises the location of your machine. (For a demonstration, visit www.anonymizer.com/cgi-bin/snoop.pl and then try typing about:global into your URL window). Intermute scrambles both your global history and cookie files, effectively covering your Internet tracks. The downside to cookie-munching programs such as Cookie Monster, Cookie Cutter or No More Cookies is that you'll no longer be able to save your shopping basket on repeat visits to Amazon.com, or skip registration to read the CyberTimes. Intermute, however, lets you maintain cookie files at select sites while protecting your anonymity at others. If you're interested in using a mixmaster remailer you can get one at the anonymizer site: www.anonymizer.com.

Responding to the vehement demand for Internet privacy at every level, Anonymizer, Inc., in San Diego, now provides anonymous dial-up connections across the United States. Anonymizer Dialup protects the user's identity no matter what they're doing. It acts as a first line of defense against attempts to track or identify people. Combined with Anonymizer's email and Anonymizer Surfing systems, Internet users can now be protected behind a double wall of iron clad security. Access Anonymizer services by visiting www.anonymizer.com. The Anonymizer Dialup service provides high-speed, unlimited Internet dialup connections in many major metropolitan areas across the United States, including San Diego, Silicon Valley, New York City, Philadelphia, Chicago and Los Angeles. The service will expand to Washington DC and several other cities in the near future. The prepaid service does not require the customer to supply any personal information. Anonymizer Dialup includes email, news groups and access to Anonymizer Surfing, which protects against threats to personal privacy while visiting web sites. Anonymizer Dialup users can connect to the Internet without revealing any personal information, even to the connection provider.

A Canadian company called ZeroKnowledge is also making anonymous Internet browsing available. They have a wide variety of services, all dedicated to keeping your privacy secure. See their site at www.zeroknowledge.com. Also check out www.grc.com for a freeware program called OptOut which checks for trojan horses attached to freeware and shareware programs you might currently be using and which send information about your computer files to a company called Aureate for marketing puposes (all without your knowledge or permission). This grc site also does a security check on your system and is a great site to have bookmarked.

There is also a product called SecureCom that is reportedly able to hide the identity of the sender and receiver of an email message along with encrypting the message itself. You might want to check out the site at www.securecominfo.com/ if you fall under the one of the following categories:

- Owners of and subscribers to email lists discussing topics that may be politically incorrect
- Contributors to Usenet-type groups, especially if topics may be politically incorrect
- Clubs and/or business associations, especially if confidential bulletins, financial statements, etc., are exchanged
- Individuals with anything 'sensitive' to communicate to others, such as communications between attorneys and clients, associates, expert witnesses, labs, etc.

- Doctors and other providers, patients, insurance companies
- Investor or business partners/associates/customers
- Political candidates and strategists
- Private investigators and clients/associates/witnesses, etc.
- Business/financial consultants and clients
- Customers and their banks/brokerage firms (e.g. wire transaction requests)
- Romantic partners
- Family members regarding personal/financial/legal matters
- Whistleblowers and one or more watchdogs or 'outside' parties
- Religious groups

New products are appearing on the market all the time. You may want to look into a product called Privacy Restored at www.zorosoft.com or NSClean at www.nsclean.com, both of which clean up your electronic paper trail (like cookies and URL history). Another called Guard Dog, does the same thing. In any event, you should take some care to "cover your tracks" or not leave any in the first place. Following some general rules and procedures will help and using an electronic vacuum to clean up traces of your wanderings is a good general way to protect yourself. If you are in an ultra sensitive position or would like the best protection, you may wish to take more proactive steps along the lines of a totally anonymous Internet service provider like Anonimizer.com.

Privacy policies

If you use a particular site regularly, you might want to inquire about their privacy policies. Let them know that privacy is important to you and ask them to publicly post their policies.

You can get a list of questions that should be answered by a privacy policy at: www.cdt.org/privacy/guide/start/privpolicy.html

Even if you are satisfied with their policy statement, don't put your complete trust in them. In August, 1998, federal regulators accused GeoCities of lying to its customers about maintaining their privacy. GeoCities gives people free space to build web sites if they answer some questions of a personal nature, including education, income, marital status, occupation, and personal interests. At the time, GeoCities was among the Internet's top 10 most popular sites. Unfortunately, they admitted that they did indeed collect and then disseminate personal information about customers to advertisers, in violation of their stated policy. Just because a company says they'll respect your privacy, doesn't mean that they will.

General privacy and security tips while online

1. Use only Internet service providers that have good privacy policies and don't sell or rent your name to others.
2. Remember your activity while online is recorded or accessible to others even though you may delete it on your computer.
3. Don't enter credit card or other personal information online unless you are sure of the site and its level of security.
4. Consider encrypting all sensitive files or email.
5. Change your password frequently and choose ones that are complex, mixing letters and numbers.
6. Never give out any identifying information, such as passwords, user name, Social Security Number, or account numbers to anyone. This information is best communicated in written form.
7. Avoid web sites that want personal information or email addresses.
8. Avoid web sites that require that you download special programs, applets, or scripts. These programs may contain viruses or Trojan horses that allow the owners of the site to gain access to or read the contents of your computer.

9. Be wary of freeware or shareware and always check for viruses before executing for the first time.
10. Avoid cookies and sites that require them. If you must use them, use a program like Cookie Cutter that allows you to pick your sites.
11. Turn off Java and Java Script, turning them back on only for selected sites that have very strict privacy policies and you know they can be trusted.
12. Be alert for changes in the operation of your computer. Watch out for anything unusual.
13. Be sure to use a "firewall" for business computers or networks. See a network security expert about various types and security levels. You should also use a firewall product if you leave your computer connected to the internet all the time as when using a cable or DSL modem.
14. Advise your children to never give out any personal information over the Internet and never to click on something that executes a program.

Trash - electronic and other

Discarded files on your computer and trash in the garbage can amount to the same security threat. Always cross-shred any identifying papers you throw away and then burn them in your fireplace if possible (followed by stirring the ashes). At least tear off the account numbers on old bills and bank statements. Its not that difficult. If you are hiding from a threatening former spouse or someone else, you will have to take more precautions, including throwing away nothing that could identify your whereabouts. You can take your trash to a dumpster somewhere or find other ways of disposing of it. You might consider archiving all documents onto optical disk and then encrypting the files, followed by shredding and/or burning the originals.

On the Job

By law, you do not have to provide a Social Security Number to be hired for most jobs. See the section on resources for information about how to succeed here. Mr. Otto Skinner's books provide information and sample letters to write in support of this. If you can be hired as an independent contractor, all the better. Most companies will want a Social Security, Social Insurance Number, or taxpayer identification number so that they can send you a 1099, but again you do not have to provide one! Mr. Skinner also provides support for refusing to divulge a Social Security Number for 1099 purposes.

Employers have even more rights to invade your privacy than law enforcement agencies. They regularly do searches on prospective employees and then continue to monitor their behavior and communications all during the work day. They can track and record your movements, your paperwork, your computer usage, your time, your conversations, everything.

If you list anyone as someone to contact "In case of emergency" don't put a name and address down for anyone you don't trust completely. In fact you may want to put down a completely bogus name. Investigators and scam artists have a way of conning information out of your friends and relatives through threats, intimidation, lies, promising rewards, or appeals to their patriotism.

Privacy waivers

You may be asked to sign a privacy waiver as a condition of employment. Carefully read any such waiver and decide if the job is worth the rights you give up. Don't just assume that the waiver is benign. You may be able to sign a modified waiver or none at all. Read the fine print. Does the waiver force you to provide your employer with anything they want and strip you of any rights to sue or refuse to cooperate?

Social Security and Social Insurance Numbers

Even though having a Social Security Number is purely voluntary, nearly all employers ask for it. You can get around this by stating you don't have one or don't use one and letting the company know the law. They still don't have to hire you if you refuse to provide the number, so don't discuss this issue until *after* you are hired. They don't need it to interview you and you should state that it's a matter of personal privacy that in general you don't reveal your Social Security Number to people. If they want to do a background check, they can do it without one. Ideally you would want to work for someone as a private contractor anyway. See if they will go for this. If you have a trust or other type of entity set up, you may be able to pledge your services to the entity and not have to provide a TIN or EIN number to anyone. In this case they would also not be required to provide you with a 1099 at the end of the year since you don't really work for them. See the resources section at the end of this book for organizations that can provide entity information.

Email, Internet browsers, and corporate networks

See section labeled "At home" for protecting yourself with regard to your computer. Everything there regarding caches, cookies, swap files, and deleted files also applies at work. You should act as if none of your work is private. At the very least, you should have your own Internet account with your own personal email address. Don't check your email from work unless you can configure the email program to not download the messages to the company computer (which does not belong to you, nor does any data on it). You should assume that *everything* you do at work belongs to the company you work for. A very large percentage of businesses these days are monitoring everything their employees do in every way.

Keyloggers are programs that reside in your computer put there deliberately (by employer, parent, anyone with access to your computer) or accidentally by you when you downloaded something from the Internet. They record what you type or what's on your screen. To check for their existence, you'll need to look in several places. Assuming you're using Windows 95/98, there are a couple of places that are the most likely. First however, you must make backup copies of any file that you change in any way. If you don't, you risk losing the ability to use your computer at all. Software currently exists that easily monitors Internet usage and can be set to track all sites visited, bookmarks, cache activity, graphics and cookies at intervals determined by the user. One product called Prudence can be configured to simply log the information or to download and encrypt all graphics, storing them in a hidden file on the user's hard drive for later scrutiny. It can also be set to email logs to the watcher, issuing an update every few minutes.

You may or may not have the authority or ability to modify your computer's configuration on the job, but if you think you do and you have the technical skill, you can use the following methods to check your machine:

In Windows 95/98 close all currently running programs (or important files) on your task bar, then press CTRL+ALT+DEL once. This will bring up the "close program" dialog box. As you look through the list of programs, note anything suspicious (the better key loggers hide themselves from this, but it's worth a try). If you don't know what the program does and it looks suspicious, take note of the name, and then select it and click end task. One such program called Keylog masks itself as Winmem in the task manager, so you won't always know. You can also press ALT+TAB noting the program names. Again, better programs also hide from this, but it's worth checking. If something looks suspicious, close it.

In Windows 3.x, use a text editor like notepad to look at C:\WINDOWS\WIN.INI. Make sure you make a backup copy of this important file before you edit it in any way. Look for two lines at the beginning of the file called LOAD and RUN. Each of these lines can be used by key logging programs to run on startup. If you see anything suspicious, put a semi-colon in front of the line (on the left). This disables the command. You may also want to take note of the file that is being run (so you can delete it later, if in fact it is a malicious program). If one of the programs you need doesn't run after this, you can always go back and remove the semi-colon.

Check your Start Menu in Win95 and Win98. There is probably a folder entitled "startup" where a key logger could be hiding. Again, look for suspicious programs and delete the shortcut from the startup menu. You may also want to check the properties of the shortcut to see what file it is running so you can delete it.

The system registry is just about the most important file in Windows 95/98 and you should not change it in any way unless you know what you are doing, and even then you should make a backup. Programs can put references in the windows registry so that they run on startup. To have a look at your registry, run REGEDIT.EXE (probably in c:\windows or c:\windows\system). Look for the key: HKEY_LOCAL_MACHINE\SOFTWARE\Microsoft\Windows\CurrentVersion\Run. Check also RunServices, RunOnce, RunOnceEx, RunServicesOnce and ShellServiceObjectDelayLoad along with Setup (one or two below the run blocks). There may also be a spurious program in the MS-DOSOptions section. Check the autoexec.bat and config.sys files as well as config.win, autoexec.syd, config.syd and MSDos.sys files too.

Finally, you might type out some obscure phrase and then use a utility program or the find utility in Windows 95/98 to search for all files with the phrase located within. It should only be in the program you used to enter it.

Keyloggers can often be defeated by programs like BOClean available at www.nsclean.com and sold by Arosoft. Other products that check for keylogger trojan horses are BlackIce Defender (www.networkice.com/) which monitors your computer at all times and eSafe Protect Desktop 2.1. See www.zdnet.com/products/stories/reviews/0,4161,410456,00.html It's a shareware product that provides firewall services, anti-virus protection, ActiveX and Java blocking, and even a "sandbox" where you can run suspect programs safely. The sandbox uses virtual device drivers, so that suspect code will run but trigger alarms if it does anything improper. The anti-virus module screens downloads and attachments on the spot. The firewall and sandbox are controlled by rule sets, which can get rather complicated. You can even tell eSafe Protect to block transmission of specific data, such as your Social Security number.

If you're really concerned about people spying on your computer you might want to do some research on Tempest, a standard for electromagnetic shielding for computer equipment. It was developed to address the threat that information might be read from a distance via emanation of radiation from computer systems, especially monitors. Military and sensitive government computers are supposed to meet Tempest specifications. You can find more information about Tempest at:

www.eskimo.com/~joelm/tempest.html
www.jya.com/emp.htm

Surveillance - audio and video

Audio and video surveillance is a fact of life at a large percentage of businesses these days. You can see video cameras everywhere and they are watching the employees as much as the customers. Actually employees steal more than shoplifters anyway. Don't assume anything you do at work is private. Don't say anything on the phone you wouldn't want repeated in a court of law. Don't assume that the rest rooms are private. If you are on company property, your behavior can and very possibly is, being recorded. Be vigilant. If you want to talk with someone in private, take a walk!

Location indicators

These are electronic devices placed on company cars allowing the company to track the vehicle's location wherever it is 24 hours a day. Modern GPS systems allow the location to be determined to within a few yards. They are usually hidden and you won't know that they even exist. There are also devices to detect speed and driving actions of all drivers using the vehicle. If you wear or carry a "smartcard" or some other form of electronic ID at work, these can also be used to monitor your physical location via sensors in doorways, walls, floors, and ceilings. Whether or not your company uses these high-tech monitors on your movements, you need to be aware of their existence and act accordingly. Companies are becoming increasingly more sophisticated and they may inform employees about the devices they are using, but probably won't. Remember that you are on company property.

Corporate espionage

You need to be aware that hackers are very busy and break-ins to corporate networks are common, though not widely acknowledged. Approximately 81% of large firms surveyed in mid 1998 said they'd found evidence of internal fraud during previous 12 months. With the advent of international electronic networks and commerce, systems are increasingly difficult to manage. Cultural differences, variances in laws, and uneven enforcement of security policies create problems even discovering security breaches. Networks Associates Inc., a company specializing in, among other things, anti-virus software, purchased a company called Secure Networks Inc., which was working on a product called Honey Pot. This product sets up a phony virtual network to lure hackers. It then traces their movements and determines their location. While it may be nice to catch a thief or competitor in the act, it's a lot better to prevent access to company secrets in the first place. Stealing corporate secrets and otherwise damaging data on competitors' systems is a reality of life that most companies still don't accept, even though it's happening every day. Even large sophisticated companies are at risk. All the major government agencies have been hacked, along with Microsoft, IBM, U.S.West, AOL, and thousands of others. America Online Inc. experienced a series of attacks during which hackers gained access to subscriber and AOL staff accounts. It appears that the intruders gained access by tricking AOL customer service representatives into resetting passwords, based on information they obtained by looking at member profiles.

Another thing you must be aware of is the problem of hackers hired by disgruntled employees or former employees in your information services department, especially those with intimate knowledge of your system and equipment. A story out of the *Dallas Morning News* in August of 1998 details how two executives at one firm were suspected of attempting to steal company secrets and customers from their employer with the intent of setting up their own competing business. Investigators found offering memos aimed at potential investors, letters to venture capitalists, and a list of clients they had planned to lure away from the company.

You *must* maintain the best security you can afford for your computers and network system! Passwords offer very little protection these days and firewalls along with physical security are an absolute must. Even if your company is not a high profile one or does not deal in sensitive products, it's important to you, your employees, and your customers. Furthermore, even a system crash could be very expensive, not to mention the time it might take to reconstruct the damage. People can become disgruntled for a wide variety of reasons. Don't take chances. Security is just a cost of doing business. Keep in mind that your company's procedures and information may be of value to competitors who might be willing to pay someone to get at them. Review your privacy policies and procedures, rethink your employee policies, and especially reevaluate your company's vulnerability in all areas. Most companies I have seen allow employees to come and go as they please with briefcases and bags that may be full of sensitive company information, including passwords and system configuration data. You don't want to run your business like a prison, but you can be sensitive to who is allowed access to the most important information and create procedures for changing security items like passwords and access codes on a regular basis.

If you're interested in ultra secure data storage you should look into the following, which are beyond the scope of this book:

- Hiding data in computer graphic files (Steganography) and the detection and jamming thereof, including detecting data in watermarks.
- Data written to unformatted floppy diskettes, 'extra' tracks, 'extra' sectors, hidden partitions, unallocated space, file slack areas.
- Data hidden in the partition gap, hidden by diffusion into binary objects and Windows swap files, and within disks.
- Floppy diskette detection of data storage anomalies.
- Encryption used in creative ways to hide entire storage devices.
- Data scrubbing of ambient data storage areas (slack, unallocated space and swap file).
- Data scrubbing of storage devices and devices that exceed the DOS 4gb limit.
- Secure erasure of files.
- Shadow data that exists after data has been overwritten.

Another thing that you need to be aware of is that owning a business is seen by the government as a privilege and having a permit is especially privileged. The Ohio Supreme Court has ruled in a 4-4 decision that law enforcement officials or state liquor agents need not identify themselves before entering and conducting a search on a business operating under a state business or liquor license. This means that if an Ohio business has a liquor license, they are not protected by the requirement of a warrant before they can be searched!

Medical Records

There are currently no federal laws protecting your right to confidentiality of medical records. There are a mish mash of state laws that attempt to protect patient rights, but these are mostly ineffective. The Medical Information Bureau is a clearing house for medical records. Whenever you receive any health assistance, you routinely sign a waiver allowing the provider to share the information with anyone with a compelling need for it and it will surely be shared with the MIB. This database was created in the early 1900's to help protect the insurance industry from applicants who might want to conceal important medical information from insurance companies and currently has data on about 15 million Americans. You can request to see your records by writing to them at:

Medical Information Bureau
PO Box 105, Essex Station
Boston, MA 02112
(617) 426-3660

Canada's equivalent bureau is at:

Medical Information Bureau
330 University Ave.
Toronto, Ontario
Canada M5G 1R7
(416) 597-0590

You can also request to see your records from your local health provider. Even though specific laws exist in only about 20 states giving you a specific right to do so, most facilities will comply with your request. Normally you'll be allowed to correct any erroneous information or to add notations to explain entries.

Errors do occur and it may be to your advantage to check your records about once a year. Because your records are available to most anyone who claims to have a right to see them, it is possible that you could be denied a job, a promotion, or insurance because of something that dates back many years. You could also find yourself getting marketing materials from pharmaceutical or other health related companies after a free cholesterol screening at the local mall. If you think you are being discriminated against because of something in your medical records or your records are being released improperly, you can contact:

U.S. Equal Opportunity Employment Commission
1801 L St., NW
Washington, DC 20507
(202) 663-4900
www.eeoc.gov

There may also be a local office. The Americans with Disabilities Act also attempts to give citizens some help in fighting discrimination due to medical conditions. The ADA specifies that employers may not ask job applicants about medical information or require a physical exam prior to offering a job and even after the job is offered, they can only ask for an exam if it's required of all employees with similar jobs. If you are denied a job or promotion based on medical conditions, your employer must prove that it is physically impossible for you to perform the job. You can contact the ADA center at:

ADA Regional Disability and Business Technical
Assistance Center
(800) 949-4232
www.pacdbtac.org

See also:
U.S. Department of Health and Human Services
Privacy Advocate

200 Independence Ave., SW
Washington, D.C. 20201

The following group sells a brochure called "Your Health Information Belongs to You" Check for cost information before ordering:

American Health Information Management Association
919 N. Michigan Ave.
Chicago, IL 60611-1683
(800) 335-5535

If you're interested in participating in the effort to strengthen medical privacy rights for patients, you can contact the following organizations who advocate for this cause:

Center for Democracy and Technology
1634 I St., NW, No. 1100
Washington, DC 20006
(202) 637-9800
www.cdt.org
Ask for their report on Privacy and Health Information Systems

National Coalition for Patient Rights
405 Waltham, No. 218
Lexington, MA 02173
(617) 861-0635

Keep in mind that if your medical records are subpoenaed, they become a public record. You can ask the court to allow only a specific portion of your medical record to be seen or not to be open at all. A judge will decide what parts, if any, of your medical record should be considered private. After the case is decided, you can also ask the judge to "seal" the court records containing your medical information. Furthermore, health care providers communicate with each other via phone, fax, and email just like you do. Cordless phones pose a threat to your privacy and you should check out your provider's policy on the use of cordless and cellular phones and fax machines when discussing and transmitting medical information. If they don't have an adequate policy, ask them to develop one. If you do not receive satisfactory answers to your questions from health providers or they do not provide you with accurate copies of your records, you should contact your local patients' rights group, the local medical society, the state medical board or an attorney. A provider may determine that releasing information in your records is damaging to you in some way and you may need legal assistance to get it. Remember, there are lots of people out there who think they know what's good for you more than you do!

You can try to limit the amount of information disseminated about you by giving only the minimum necessary when you receive any medical care. You can also change the customary waiver for authorization to release all of your medical information by writing that you only authorize releasing specific records pertaining to the current condition and only for the treatment or advise you're getting from specific doctors or facilities on certain dates. Always assume that your doctor/patient relationship is public record, *not* private. Especially be aware of company sponsored health care providers. Regardless of who you use, never talk about any high-risk sports or activities you may engage in with any health care provider, (unless of course you are obviously suffering from an injury or illness caused by that activity)! If you are injured because of such an activity, it may be impossible to avoid such a disclosure, but you certainly don't have to volunteer it in the normal course of dealing with people connected to the health care industry. Don't assume that the information is confidential even if you only relate it casually at a free screening at a local mall.

The only way you can gain some privacy at this time is to visit a hospital, clinic, or doctor/dentist and not reveal your Social Security/Social Insurance Number. If they say that they need your records, there is a company called Conquest that can request your medical records and will interpret them for you in a manner you can understand. They then give you a copy, along with a card showing any allergies or other emergency information needed in a crisis. The next time you go in for any healthcare somewhere, they will provide only the information necessary for the current problem, thereby respecting your privacy and not revealing ancient events in your records that may have nothing to do with your current condition. They are staffed by emergency care physicians who are available over the telephone. You can look them up on the Internet at www.conquesthealth.com. Tell them you heard about them in this book. They are among a growing number of professionals interested in helping you maintain your privacy, your dignity, and your rights. Conquest also has a health assurance plan.

In the U.S. if the Clinton administration and Congress has its way, any visit to a health care provider will soon require your national ID number. If the ID scheme isn't stopped, you can probably expect to see an underground of doctors and dentists to develop who will care for you without it, but imagine the hassle. See the section on resources available at the end of this book for how to establish an anonymous identity if have a need for this. If you pay the bill and do not commit fraud, it is perfectly legal at this time to receive medical care and not reveal who you are. This may be changing however, depending on the interpretation of new legislation being proposed. The law may be changed to make illegal the use of any ID that doesn't meet certain issuance requirements.

Telecommunications

Joshua Quittner writes in the August 1997 issue of *Time* how someone "forwarded my home telephone number to an out-of-state answering machine, where unsuspecting callers trying to reach me heard a male voice identify himself as me and say some extremely rude things." He goes on to describe how the hacker asked people to leave their messages. To his surprise, many people did, including his mother. This went on for six months in spite of efforts by the phone company, unlisted numbers, PIN codes, and traces! The hacker kept breaking through somehow! Some things that could have happened include: recording conversations or email, calling in his mortgage, discontinuing health insurance, destroying his good credit history, sending bogus calls to superiors, adding false judgments to his credit report, inserting arrest records or convictions to public records, destroying his future ability to get a job. Think this couldn't happen to you? Think again! The least you should do is to get an unlisted number for your home. This won't stop dedicated pranksters, but is a good beginning and should be considered a minimum effort to protect your privacy.

Faxes can be intercepted. If the receiving, intercepting, and sending fax systems have hands-on telephone sets, it is even possible that the conversation in the room of the sending fax can be heard during transmission. Consider the implications of any faxing you do. Some fax machines come with secure "mail boxes". These at least require a code to be entered before someone can print out the faxes held for the intended person. You may want to reconsider private couriers like UPS and FedEx for sensitive documents.

Voice Mail is a recording! According to *Privacy Times*, 85% or more of all corporations use voice mail, along with 40-45% of households in the U.S. Do you have your own answering machine with a tape or digital recorder or do you use a telephone company's voice mail? When you delete a message from your voice mail, do you know what happens to it? You should never trust the phone company (or any other company) to protect your personal information! Always use your own answering machine, even though it may break or not have the same services as you can get with the phone company. At least you are in physical control of it and can truly destroy messages after use (even if you have to destroy the machine). Remember, convenience is often at the root of loss of privacy.

When it comes to voice mail at work, don't forget who owns it. Your employer does! Secondly, don't forget who can get to it, including hackers, other employees within the company, people outside the company, or former employees. A story in the *Washington Post* about Chiquita in July of 1998, reported that a reporter from *The Enquirer* recorded conversations between himself and Chiquita attorneys, during which he asked them questions about allegations that they secretly control other banana companies, spray dangerous pesticides on workers and villagers in Central America, and that they attempted to bribe Colombian officials. He then reportedly was able to obtain the voice mail recordings of these same attorneys as they discussed drafting answers to his questions with company officials. More than 2000 voice mail messages, mostly from the legal department, were recorded.

Chiquita found, to its dismay, that this supposedly secure communication, could be stolen and published in a major newspaper (in this case on the pages of the Sunday *Cincinnati Enquirer*). Where would you like a copy of *your* voice mail to be published? If you're an individual, concerned about your privacy, be sure to keep your voice mail on your own machine and even then be careful about what you say. If you own or work for a company, there needs to be strict security policies in place for voice mail and email. Even then these policies and procedures need to be tested regularly as part of a routine security maintenance program.

800 Numbers - The company who owns the 800 number finds out who is calling because they are the ones who pay the bill. So, just like on a regular phone bill, all toll-free phone calls are logged. Have you ever noticed how a company asks you for your name and address when you call an 800 number? The next time you call, they often answer the phone and ask whether this is Mr. or Mrs. Doe. They know you because the number you are calling from flashes on their screen before they even answer the phone. There is NO way to block your phone number from being transmitted to the company that owns the 800 number, so don't ask. Every time you call an 800 number, you give them your phone number. All of the above also applies to 888 and 877 toll-free numbers.

If a private investigator for instance, wants to track down a dead beat, they might advertise or otherwise contact a suspect by offering something for which the person needs to call an 800 number. They would have a different extension for each person they are trying to find so that they could instantly know who it was who called. Some pretext messages that get called back include prize winner notification, unclaimed money in an old bank account, and offers of new credit cards or extension of additional credit. They might also use revocation of credit privileges, telephone services, courier package delivery, confirming a mail order for a product, or to retrieve a "phone telegram". It is illegal to use the name of government agencies or other companies, with which they are not affiliated, but they might be creative and use a similarly sounding name.

Use toll-free numbers with discretion. Remember they are used for marketing purposes. Never call one from your secure phone. If you do make a call, ask if the company will refrain from any follow-up marketing efforts. If necessary, call from a phone booth.

All numbers of local and long distance calls are recorded by the phone company. A person impersonating a phone company employee can trick real employees into divulging the long distance calls, but it usually takes a contact on the inside, within the security department, to get at the local calls, because these don't appear on the operator's screens. If someone doesn't have your phone number already, they only need to call the local cable company or utility. Its easy to get them to reveal the phone number of a customer by just impersonating the subject and saying you want to confirm that the number is correct. Employees will often reveal the address too. Then they take that information and go to the phone company with it to get your call history. Don't be discouraged, there are steps you can take to improve your privacy, even on the telephone. Since we all use the telephone so much, it's not really an option to just stop using it.

What can you do?

1. Ask the phone company, the cable company, and all your other utilities to refrain from giving out *any* information about you without confirming your identity first. If you need to have a code for this, set one up with them.
2. If you need extra security because you're being stalked or harassed by someone, you may want to have your phone and other utilities under someone else's name or in the name of a trust. You could also use an alternate identity if you have supporting documents. They usually want a Social Security Number or driver's license number.
3. See if the phone and utility companies will take a cash deposit and not use your credit card.
4. If you do give your name as the customer, give them a mail drop or secretarial service address. Still ask them to refrain from giving out your personal information without verification of your identity.
5. Don't say anything on a cellular or cordless phone that you wouldn't want heard in a court of law, written up in the papers, or put on a billboard.
6. Don't say your phone card number aloud when others are around. If you use a calling card, stand close to the phone or use your hands to conceal the buttons when you enter the number and the PIN. Same thing goes for using your ATM card.
7. Never get mail at home. Anything that comes in your name, mark "wrong address" and send it back unopened.
8. Use a post office or private mail box for official correspondence (even credit related business). A private mail box or secretarial service is preferred over the U.S. Postal Service.
9. Use a mail drop (private mail box) established in a trust name or an anonymous name. You can use a local one or get one in a foreign jurisdiction. Do <u>not</u> use the U.S. Postal Service! See references section for secretarial services or

mail drops that are private and can forward mail. For really serious cases, you can use 2 or 3 mail drops forwarding mail from one to another until it finally gets to the one you pick up mail from. This causes a delay, but may be worth it. Information on mail drops is also available from privacy groups like PMI Enterprises.

10. Use courier services for sensitive documents and avoid the postal service. FBI and other government agencies like the NSA and CSE have chemicals they can spray on envelopes that allow them to read mail without opening the envelope. They are also good at opening and resealing envelopes or removing the contents without disturbing the seal. The U.S. and Canadian Postal Services cooperate fully with them in this.
11. Be careful what you say on either digital or analog phones.
12. Use the lock feature on your cellular phone when its not in service
13. Be careful who has access to your cell phone. Don't leave it in your car when a valet is parking it, or when you take it to a mechanic or a car wash.
14. Never believe someone who says they need to "test the line" on your cell phone. There is no "line".
15. Report frequently interrupted or dropped cell calls. Someone who has cloned your phone may be interrupting your calls.
16. Check your phone bills carefully for unknown or unusual activity.
17. Ask your cellular carrier what anti-fraud features are available and then use them. Some companies will automatically watch for unusual activity and notify you. You may also be able to acquire special PIN numbers to lock out criminals.
18. Keep documents containing your cell phone's serial number and other information in a secure place.
19. Report a stolen or lost cell phone immediately to your cellular carrier.
20. Don't fax sensitive documents unless you encrypt them.

21. Make toll-free calls from other phones, using a prepaid card, or your cell phone (especially if your cell phone is a prepaid one that you can get with no ID). Caller ID blocking doesn't work on 800, 888, and 877 toll-free calls or sometimes other long-distance numbers. Your long distance carrier will give you away.
22. Use encryption in all email of any sensitivity. Don't ever say anything important in the subject line or the first 2 lines of the message. Get a good encryption program and then trade passwords with the person you wish to communicate with, but do it in person.
23. Use anonymous browsing and email on the Internet with a program like Anonymizer or ZeroKnowledge.
24. Watch what you say in general. Don't brag about trusts or off-shore accounts you may have. Be discreet and maintain a low profile.

More information and support is available from:

Federal Communications Commission Enforcement Division
2025 M Street, NW
Washington, D.C. 20054
(202) 418-0569
www.fcc.gov

Paging and Narrowband PCS Alliance
500 Montgomery St., No. 700
Alexandria, VA 22314
(703) 739-0300

Cellular Telecommunications Industry Association
1250 Connecticut Avenue, NW, No. 200
Washington, D.C. 20036
(202) 785-0081
www.wow-com.com

Electronic Industries Association
2500 Wilson Blvd.
Arlington, VA 22201
(703) 907-7500
www.eia.org

Personal Communications Industry Association
500 Montgomery St., No. 700
Alexandria, VA 22314
(703) 739-0300
www.pcia.com

Equipment vulnerability

Cordless phones are about the same as yelling out the window. They are easily monitored by scanners or even other cordless phones, radios, and baby monitors. All of this equipment, plus pagers, home intercom systems, and walkie-talkies can be monitored from as far away as two miles by scanners you can get locally. It's estimated that there are 10-15 million scanner owners in the U.S. There are many people who routinely listen in for entertainment or think its their patriotic duty to monitor calls and notify the police if they hear anything that "might" be considered illegal. Don't say anything on a cordless phone that you wouldn't want said in a court of law. The newer phones which use the higher 900 megahertz frequency and have as many as 30 to 100 channels are also vulnerable to eavesdropping. Remember to tell all members of the family that they need to be careful with what they say on a cordless phone. Children need to be taught that they don't reveal phone numbers or addresses on a cordless phone. If you tell them that everyone in the neighborhood might be able to hear what they say, they will probably be very willing to cooperate. You might also inform your friends and relatives who may not be aware of this problem.

Cellular phone conversations can be intentionally or accidentally listened to from as far away as ten miles with a good scanner. Robin Rimbaud, an English artist, musician, and publisher, has released three albums mixing music and overheard cellular phone transmissions. There is even an audio underground where taped cellular calls are illegally copied and disseminated as entertainment. It has become so widespread, that even the FBI and phone company executives have had their phone conversations recorded and their phones cloned. Most of the time the victim has no idea either activity is going on. Federal law prohibits intentional eavesdropping, but the problem is proving intent. The person may say that it was perfectly accidental. The FCC ruled that as of April 1994, no scanners can be manufactured or imported that can tune into frequencies used by cellular phones or be readily altered to pick up those frequencies. The trouble is that there are plenty of old scanners still being used that have these capabilities and electronics magazines or the Internet have plenty of help in making the alterations necessary or buying older ones.

Furthermore, using a cloning device, a person can scan the airwaves and pick up your cell phone's electronic serial number. They can then install that number into their own (often stolen) phones and the calls will be billed to you. Worse yet, you do not even have to be using your phone for it to be cloned, it just has to be turned on. Cloners like to frequent busy highways or downtown locations where lots of cell phones are in use. The cloning business is very big and growing every day. According to the Cellular Telecommunications Industry Association, the cellular industry loses almost $500 million a year to fraud, including cloning. Estimates range to nearly $1 billion a year, and growing. New York, California, and Florida are the three biggest markets for cellular fraud, especially Florida, because of its flat terrain and the high use of cell phones there. If your phone has been cloned, it will need to be reprogrammed to prevent further charges to your bill. By the way, cloning is not always easy to detect. Sometimes criminals will spread calls around so as to reduce the likelihood that you will notice anything unusual on your bill until a long time has transpired. Then it is too late and you'll have paid the bills already. It's a federal crime to use a cloned phone, and the FBI investigates this problem, but they mostly go after manufacturers and large scale cloning operations. At this time, you'll just have to keep your cellular phone turned off whenever its not needed, and *always* check your bills.

Digital phones and PCS devices (Personal Communication Services) are a combination of cell phone, email, and pager and use digital technology to send and receive calls. At this time digital phones and PCS devices suffer from some coverage limitations, so ask about this when you're shopping around and comparing the benefits of analog vs. digital. Get an encrypted analog phone for privacy. PCS's and digital phones are easily tapped. It has also been revealed that the phone number is made available on the internet for strangers to peruse (without your permission of course).

Pagers, home intercoms, baby monitors, and walkie-talkies are similar in vulnerability to cordless phones as they all use frequencies on the airwaves that are easily picked up by scanners or even other similar devices. You should observe the same precautions when using these devices as you would with a cordless phone. Warn your children too! Its currently illegal to intercept messages from display or voice pagers, but not from tone-only ones.

Eavesdropping and wire tapping are not things that only threaten spies and embassies. You can be a target too, especially if you have an ex-spouse or a disgruntled employee. If your phone *is* tapped, you will need to call a security professional to discuss your options. It is also possible for a phone to be tapped so that someone can listen in even with the receiver on the hook. This is called a hookswitch bypass, and turns your phone into a listening device that can detect sounds all over your house. Call a professional from a pay phone and don't identify yourself until you have discussed your situation. Make arrangements for their services in a secure manner. You may have to physically go to their location to make these arrangements. You will not be able to defeat a federal wiretap, but you can have a professional TSCM sweep done and invest in encryption equipment for both your phone and your fax machine.

If you don't think that your phone would ever be wiretapped because you're a law-abiding citizen, you need to know about a practice called "the hand-off." It was first discovered in Los Angeles by defense attorneys involved in a cocaine possession case. Possibly hundreds of thousands of phone conversations between law-abiding citizens were being monitored and recorded, then kept on file for at least nine years (NSA policy). In fact, it was discovered that the LAPD has been sharing confidential wiretap information between department personnel since 1984, without court permission or supervisory oversight. Here's how "the hand-off" works: detectives go to a judge and make a case for probable cause against a person, let's call him Joe. The wiretap is authorized, but only for a short period of time, like 40 days. Now investigators are required to file reports every 72 hours detailing whether and why the tap should be allowed to continue, but this is commonly ignored. The judge is required to sign off on that order, every 72 hours. After 90 days, the law requires that anyone who has been overheard, must be notified of the tap in writing by the investigative agency.

Now if a conversation is picked up between Joe and another person or between two people unrelated to the original investigation, and the conversation even suggests a new, unrelated illegal activity is or may take place, then the investigators merely "hand-off" this recording to another team who will start a whole new investigation. The "evidence" from the recording is presented to a new judge who is then convinced to issue a new wiretap. The problem is that the investigators never mention where they got the "evidence" from for this new wiretap. Even if the matter goes to court, the district attorney never reveals to the defense attorney anything about the source of the "evidence" that resulted in the new wiretap. Of course then the defense attorney does not have all the information needed to mount a sufficient defense or even to conduct his own investigation or ask pertinent questions in the discovery phase of a trial, as is required by law.

In addition, it has been found from the details of the above case, that wiretaps often last much longer than the 40 days allowed by law. The requirements for continuously reporting, evaluating and re-authorizing wiretaps every 72 hours also seems to be routinely ignored. The wiretap law in California clearly specifies that unrelated information obtained as the result of a wiretap cannot and in fact, should not, be used to open separate investigations. California's Attorney General is required by law to provide a complete accounting and report to the California State Legislature and state Judicial Council of the total number and complete duration of any and all wiretaps carried out by any state law enforcement agency in April of each year. You may be surprised at how many Aprils go by without this report being produced.

Even the Administrative Office of United States Courts, the agency charged with overseeing all "authorized" federal wiretaps estimates that, in federal cases, only about 20% of all "monitored" conversations involve discussions of criminal activity. In spite of this figure, your public servants find it to be their prerogative to spy on you without legal authorization. If you are *ever* prosecuted and the case involves any kind of wiretap, your defense team needs to actively look into violation of law and procedures by local, state, and federal law enforcement. There are currently class action lawsuits pending that address this illegal practice of "hand-offs". Furthermore, the federal government has decided that in the digital age, it is becoming too expensive to conduct regular wiretaps and has demanded that telephone companies make it easier to tap your phone. Half a billion dollars was authorized in 1994 to support phone companies in this effort. Since then the amount paid to the phone companies was reduced and they are suing the federal government for more money to complete the "upgrade". Regardless of who pays the tab, it eventually all comes back to you in the form of taxes or phone bills.

You can protest to your congressman or woman or to local council members if you find the same thing happening in your town, but you can rest assured, if you don't protest and the practice isn't challenged, it will continue. You can also protest to the courts and the attorney general's office. They are elected officials and care about their jobs.

Telephone company employees may legally listen in on your conversations when they deem it necessary to provide you with service, to inspect the system, to monitor the quality of the service, or to help "protect you" from service theft or harassment. Keep in mind also that employers can listen in on and record all employee calls (and email). In most states it is illegal to tape-record phone conversations and where it is legal, most states require that both parties know and that there be a distinguishing beep tone to indicate the recording. If one party lives in a state where only one party needs to provide the consent and the other party lives in a 2-party consent state, the federal law of 1-party consent applies, so don't assume that you are protected. These regulations don't apply to law-enforcement or emergencies however. The FCC admits that the law is difficult to enforce and you should never assume that your conversation is *not* being recorded. Be aware that your phone may be tapped and conversations recorded without a court order under the so-called "one-party consent provision" which allows a tap with the consent of only one party. This is how Linda Tripp was able to legally record her conversations with Monica Lewinsky. The consenting party may be a government informant or someone recently recruited to be an informant. This law only applies to eavesdropping by law-enforcement officials however.

If you suspect your phone or residence is being tapped:

1. Be careful with what you say! Warn others who also might use your phone!
2. Do not call some purported number someone gives you to check to see if it *is* tapped, listening for clicks, sirens, or other such nonsense. Many security professionals have debunked this popular myth. There is no way you can determine if your phone is tapped merely by calling a number.
3. Contact a professional security company to have a TSCM sweep conducted. Don't rely on equipment you find down at a local electronics store. Most is junk, doesn't work, and will give you a false sense of security.
4. If you do buy equipment, you'll want professional quality gear, found at stores that sell to security professionals. Beware that tap tracing equipment may or may not work or may give false positives. They often claim to work by detecting voltage drops in the system, but normal fluctuations could cause the same thing. They are also ineffective in a business environment where a switchboard and multiple lines exist. Professional encryption devices are the only way to assure security, since, even if you do find and disable a tap, it can be reinstalled.
5. Use prepaid phone cards. The places you call are not listed on your phone bill, but complete privacy is not guaranteed however as the origin of the call to the 800 number is still recorded and available to law enforcement agencies. For complete privacy, you'd have to place these calls from a phone booth and even then, if you are a high profile person, or are being pursued by the police, they can use voice print analysis to detect who you are.
6. Use a voice mailbox and have callers leave messages. You later call in, retrieve the messages and call the people you want to talk to. You can even get an inexpensive voice mailbox without giving out any identifying information. Using

this, especially in combination with an alias name and a mail drop is an excellent way to screen calls. See the section on resources for where to find these services.

7. If you fax confidential documents, you might consider a fax machine with a "keylock" and sending to machines that require codes to be entered to print out faxes for certain recipients.

Remember that not everyone obeys the laws. Even law enforcement agencies have been caught bending the law or disregarding it altogether.

Telemarketers

It is possible to stop most telemarketing to your home phone, but probably not to your business phone unless all calls to your desk go through a receptionist. You can even collect fines from violators of your privacy rights such as $500.00 for each unwanted phone call or fax you receive and up to $1500.00 if the telemarketer knowingly breaks the law. The elderly are particularly susceptible to telemarketers, but everyone should follow these rules to help stop telemarketing calls:

1. Never deal with anyone who demands that you mail them a certified or cashier's check immediately. For that matter, don't have anything to do with any propositions from any telemarketers, you'll only make the problem worse.
2. Get an unlisted/unpublished number.
3. Use "Number blocking" so people you call cannot see your number.
4. Use "Anonymous Call Rejection" to block any incoming calls that fail to show their number on a caller ID screen.
5. Use "Caller ID" to display the number of anyone calling you. You can also use this number if you have to file a complaint.
6. Remember too, you can always hang up on a telemarketer.

If a telemarketer does not follow legal guidelines, you should contact your local telephone company, your state attorney general's office, the Federal Communications Commission, (888-CALL-FCC, www.fcc.gov) and the Federal Trade Commission (202-326-2222, www.ftc.gov)

Debt collectors

These people will use just about any method they can devise to track people down. If you have secured debt like a car loan, they will try to find out where you park the car, either at work or home and then send someone out to tow it away at 4:00 in the morning. They, like private investigators have a variety of methods to locate people and often follow the "paper trail" that most folks leave when they go about their daily business. They may also be hassling you for a debt you don't owe as may be the case if a debt has already been discharged in a bankruptcy or if your identity has been stolen or borrowed by someone else and the creditor is still coming after you. Skip tracers can be very creative and often have friends or contacts in the phone companies (especially in the security department). If they don't, they can still get the toll calls from your phone by using a ruse in which they claim to be from another department or from the same phone company, but in another state or city and ask for a favor from the operator in the locale where they think the subject lives. If they have the phone number, they just ask for the toll calls occurring within a certain time period. If you're being unfairly or illegally harassed by bill collectors, get an unpublished, unlisted number, caller ID, and anonymous call block. Report them to the authorities if necessary.

Harassing calls

You may or may not know the perpetrator of the call. It may be completely random. If it happens more than once or on a regular basis, it can be very disturbing, especially to women living alone. Here are a number of things you can do, not necessarily in order of priority:

1. Hang up
2. Use an answering machine to screen calls and use a message like the following:
3. "We have been receiving annoying calls and the phone company has put a trace on this line. If you do not leave a message we will assume the you are the annoyance caller and this call will be traced."
4. If you answer the phone and the harassing caller is on the other line, you might say "Operator, this is the call." Then wait a couple of seconds and hang up.
5. You might also say the word "trap" when the harasser calls. You then say the date and time and hang up. Traps and tracing can be set up on phones through the phone company, but traps require that you to keep a date and time log. Both may incur fees. The phone company supposedly does not listen to or record your conversations when a trap or trace is established.
6. Use *69 to hear the number of the last caller (if this service is available from your carrier) and then give the number to the police (or to a private investigator).
7. Use caller ID or call block to see the caller's number (and maybe also the name) and to block any calls from phones that don't allow their numbers to be displayed.
8. You might also be able to subscribe to a service that allows only calls from certain numbers to get through. This would also prevent legitimate emergency calls from getting through, so it may not be the best option.
9. There may be a service whereby a caller has to enter a digital code for the call to go through. You would have to give this code to all people you would possibly want to get calls from and again it would preclude emergency calls from getting through from those who may need to reach you, but don't know the code.

10. At lease don't mention your name and number on your answering machine message.
11. Don't give out your phone number just because some one asks for it. Alternatively you might give out a bogus number.

You may still not catch the person if they use phone booths or a variety of phones to call from, so it may just be necessary to get an unlisted, unpublished phone.

General rules and tools of telephone privacy

1. Become familiar with and use all the services available to you from your local phone company, such as caller ID, call blocking, selective blocking, complete blocking, anonymous call rejection, call tracing, inbound call blocker (this requires callers to dial special code numbers when calling you), distinctive ring (different rings for different numbers coming in on the same phone), and voice mail.
2. Use an answering machine to screen calls. It is recommended however, that you use your own answering machine, rather than the telephone company's service to keep the calls and messages on some physical device that you control. Even though the phone company records the numbers of all incoming and outgoing calls to your phone, at least they won't have the recorded messages people leave for your ears only.
3. If you suspect eavesdropping or wiretapping, you can talk to surveillance experts or private investigators (see your Yellow Pages) and use their services or devices. You can buy effective encryptors and voice modifiers to keep your calls private. You'll probably be paying in the $2-3000 price range.
4. You might look into phone security devices sold by specialty stores or on the Internet.
5. You could get an entirely new number and not have it published or listed with directory assistance.

6. You could also get a private phone number from a voice mail service. These will take calls or forward them to another phone.
7. You could consider making and receiving confidential calls away from home or work. If you don't use a voice modifier though, government voice analyzers can still identify you. Most people are not going to require this level of sophistication however.
8. You can use prepaid calling cards, or a prepaid cellular phone that has no record of your name, address, or any other identifying information, but just be careful not to reveal this while on a call. Their location can be determined, and again your voice can be analyzed, but this is only going to be done by high-level government agencies. Don't be a high-profile person and attract that kind of attention.

Telephone book and reverse directories

All names and addresses listed in the white pages of a phone directory are considered public information. Mailing list companies compile this information and sell it. The phone company and others also compile reverse directories (also known as crisscross directories) which are indexed by address and phone number rather than by name. Someone can then look up an address and find the person or company's phone number and name. Internet people finders like Yahoo use these directories. You can request an unlisted number and also request that the phone company remove your listing from its "street-address directory." There are 2 major directory companies. You should write them requesting that they remove your name from their lists.

Haines & Company, Inc.
Criss-Cross Directory

Attn. Director of Data Processing
8050 Freedom Ave., NW
N. Canton, OH 44720
(800) 562-8226

R.L. Polk & Co.
Attn: List Suppression File
26955 Northwestern Highway
South Field, MI 48034
(810) 728-7000

The Postal Service

The post office is *not* a friend to those seeking anonymity. They regularly sell change of address information to marketing companies. Don't use a change of address form when you move. Communicate your new address privately to all those who need to know and to no one else. This will *not* stop junk mail however, as millions of pieces of mail are delivered to "occupant" or "resident". You'll just have to throw this away (as is done with 44% of all junk mail - before opening). As a matter of fact, over 68 billion pieces of unsolicited mail are delivered to people each year. That's over 32 pounds per person per year! The typical consumer is on 25 to 100 marketing databases with over 22,000 different types of specialized mailing lists available to the direct marketing industry. Don't write to the companies sending it to you and ask to be taken off the list, as that will just put you *on* the list. You *can* refuse any mail. Just don't open it. Write "Return to Sender" and place in any mail box.

As far as your location is concerned, there are all kinds of ways of getting your address and your phone number (both of which are of course indexed with the other) It is even possible for a private investigator to get the name and address of a box holder. If you want to be private, use a commercial mail box drop with or without an alternate ID. Your home address is not private and neither is the mail that gets delivered there. While common thieves are able to make off with the contents of any unlocked mail box, government agencies or others with an agenda against you may just want to read your mail and then let you have it. The FBI and other agencies have methods of treating envelopes with chemicals so that they can read the contents without opening them. They are also very good at steaming open envelopes or otherwise opening and resealing them. There are also devices which can extract the contents of an envelope without opening it. They work by rolling the contents up on a type of knitting needle and then pulling it out the space that isn't sealed. You can partly thwart these attempts by wrapping the contents in aluminum foil or black paper, by sealing the flap with cellophane tape, or by enclosing the contents in another envelope and putting that in the addressed envelope. If you use non-permanent magic marker for the address and also for the letter or document, any attempts at reading the contents by using chemicals will cause the ink to run and be an obvious indication of mail tampering.

Chain letters

These are usually started with names rented from lists of opportunity seekers. You'll probably just have to throw them away, as answering them will just perpetuate the problem. When you move, you'll automatically see a reduction in all kinds of junk mail if you don't fill out a change of address form at the post office and don't give out your new address to every Tom, Dick and Harry who asks for it.

Mail fraud, theft, and tampering

These are problems you need to know exist so you can protect yourself from becoming a victim. As far as mail fraud is concerned, you need to research who you do business with and remember that stings are set up by private investigators or government agencies. Buyer beware applies here as it does with anything. Using the methods discussed in this manual, hopefully you won't be receiving fraudulent mail offers. If you use the methods in this book, you'll generally get fewer of these. You can help protect yourself from mail theft and tampering by using mail drops, ie. a post office box at a local retail outlet like Mail Boxes Etc., a locking mailbox, or a mail slot in your door. At least no one will be able to drive along the street and steal or tamper with your mail.

Mailing lists, mail order catalogs and magazines

Unfortunately there is no single source of junk mail. There are a few major companies however that you can write to in an effort to have your name removed. Keep in mind though that you'll have to repeat your efforts because your name will reappear on their lists and have to be purged again. One problem is that your name is shared between many companies and responding to one offer will get you mail or offers from others.

You can remove yourself from most national mailing lists by writing to:

> Direct Marketing Association
> Mail Preference Service
> Box 9008
> Farmingdale, NY 11735-9008

Ask them to remove you from all lists and refrain from adding your name in the future. They will put you into their computerized "purge" file. This is sent to about 3600 organizations several times a year. You should see a reduction in your junk mail, but it may take a few months. Don't expect to see all your junk mail go away though. Membership in the DMA is voluntary and many organizations don't belong. If you're still receiving mail in 5 or 6 months, you'll have to notify the individual companies. A sample letter is on the following page.

Dear Sir/Madam:

Please include me in your "Opt-Out" service and remove or block my name, address, telephone, and fax number from all mailing, telephone, and fax lists that you compile, own, rent, manage, or otherwise access. Please also make sure that I'm on any merge-purge list which you might provide for people who do not wish to receive unsolicited mail or phone calls.

I do not wish for my name, address, phone, or fax number to be given out to or used by any direct marketing companies, mailing list brokers, publishers, credit bureaus, credit card companies, banks, insurance companies or bureaus, government agencies, or any other company or organization without my written permission.

Please confirm your receipt of this letter in writing. Thank-you.

Name
Address
City/State/Zip
Phone
Fax
Signed ____________________
Dated ____________________

This same letter can be used for DMA or for individual marketing companies.

Other companies that compile and rent lists are below (you'll have to write to each one separately):

R.L. Polk & Co.
List Compilation/Opt-Out Coordinator
26955 Northwestern Highway
South Field, MI 48034
(810) 728-7000

Metromail Corp.
List Maintenance
901 West Bond
Lincoln, NE 68521
(800) 426-8901

First Data Info-Source
Donnelley Marketing, Inc.
Data Base Operations
1235 "N" Ave.
Nevada, IA 50201
(888) 633-4402

Experian
Target Marketing Services Division
Attn: Consumer Opt Out
P.O. Box 919
Allen, TX 75013
(800) 353-0809

Database America
Compilation Department
100 Paragon Dr.
Montvale, NJ 07645
(800) 223-7777

Trans Union
Name Removal Option

P.O. Box 97328
Jackson, MS 39288-7328
(800) 680-7293

Acxiom Corporation
Attn: Opt-outs/Consumer Advocacy
P.O. Box 2000
Conway, AR 72033-2000

American Business Information, Inc.
Attn: Product Quality
P.O. Box 27347
Omaha, NE 68127

You can help prevent junk mail by forbidding companies from selling or sharing your name with others. Include a separate letter with your magazine subscription that tells them not to rent, sell, share, or trade your name, address, or phone with anyone else. Be sure to sign your letter. Do this when you order from a catalog, join an organization, or get involved in anything by mail.

Card offers

Warranty cards

Most of the time these cards are not sent to the company that sold you the product, but instead to a company in Denver called National Demographics and Lifestyles Co. This company compiles buyer profiles and sells the information to others for marketing purposes. Keep your receipt and take your purchase back to where you purchased it from to obtain a refund or exchange. If you think you must send in the card, include only the least information you can, including your name, address and serial number for the product. Ask to be removed from National Demographics mailing list by writing to them at:

National Demographics and Lifestyles Co.
List Order Department
1621 18th St., No. 300
Denver, CO 80202
(800) 525-3533

Credit card/insurance/financial offers

These usually come from the mailing lists sold by the credit reporting agencies. If you are not using your Social Security Number anymore or are not using any credit that requires it, your current address will not be on the lists (assuming you have moved and not left a forwarding address with the post office). You'll need to write to each company separately and ask them to refrain from selling or sharing your name and address.

Supermarket and other retail club cards

Supermarket scanners are increasingly being used to track consumer's buying habits, especially if they use credit or debit cards. All of your information is instantly available and your new purchases immediately go into the expanding database you have been unknowingly developing. Stores like Price-Costco which require membership cards may use this information to send you solicitations and/or sell/rent your name to companies they do business with or to most any marketing company that will buy it. You may be able to request that they not distribute your name or send you junk mail. You may however just have to avoid such stores or pay cash at stores that use scanners.

Political/non-profit/charitable organizations

Because donor lists are extremely valuable, political and charitable organizations often sell or rent their lists. You can request that they not distribute your name. The problem is that they often rent these lists from companies and therefore can't delete your name. You may have to contact the company that they got your name from. The code for that company may be on the mailing label your name is on and you may have to send it in with your request so they can track down where it came from. Give anonymously so you aren't bombarded with repeat solicitations. This is especially true for colleges, universities, and political organizations. Send them cash or a money order! Never give them your name and address! If you are solicited over the phone, tell them you NEVER give to charities that solicit this way and they will have to send you something in the mail. Then, don't give them your address. If you have to hang up on them, do so.

Sweepstakes and contests

Sweepstakes and contests exist for one reason only and that is marketing. You are absolutely going to be added to a mailing list somewhere and most likely many lists if you enter often. Don't ever enter contests that require a name and address or any other kind of identifying information. Don't use mail-in rebates either. They amount to the same thing and are used for one purpose: to get your name and address! Contests are especially dangerous for elderly people because they are often fronts for scams. These schemes often require money to be sent up front for the purpose of mailing or handling costs. Every year thousands of elderly folks fall victim to these seductive contests and gimmicks. The money required for processing the "winnings" is always more than the value of the prize. If you are receiving mailings from the following, you can write to them to have your name removed:

Publisher's Clearinghouse
101 Channel Drive
Port Washington, NY 11050
(800) 645-9242

Reader's Digest
Attn: Sweepstakes
Reader's Digest Rd.
Pleasantville, NY 10570
(800) 234-9000

American Family Publishers
Box 62000
Tampa, FL 33662
(800) 237-2400

Coupon and resident mailers

You'll have to track down where the coupons or "resident" mailing came from. Look for an address or company name near your address or near the bulk rate postage mark. In your letter asking them to stop sending you mailings, you might want to include your mailing label. Always sign your written request. It may take more than one letter. You might also ask your letter carrier to refrain from delivering mail to you if it doesn't have your actual name and address on it. The major mailers are:

First Data Info-Source
Donnelley Marketing, Inc.
Data Base Operations
1235 "N" Ave.
Nevada, IA 50201
(888) 633-4402

Harte-Hanks (Pennysaver or Potpourri)
2830 Orbiter St.
Brea, CA 92821
(800) 422-4116

ADVO, Inc.
List Service Department
239 West Service Rd.
Hartford, CT 06120
(860) 520-3357

Val-Pak Coupons
Direct Marketing
P.O. Box 13428
St. Petersburg, FL 33733

Carol Wright/Cox Direct
P.O. Box 13428
St. Petersburg, FL 33733

The mail-order industry is represented by the following, where you can lodge a complaint:

Mail Order Action Line
Direct Marketing Association
1111 19th St. NW, No. 1100
Washington, D.C. 20036
(202) 955-5030

You can also write to the following groups for support and help in slowing your receipt of junk mail:

Stop Junk Mail Association
3020 Bridgeway, No. 150
Sausalito, CA 94965
(800) 827-5549
Fee-based group attempts to reduce your solicitations.

Zero Junk Mail
405 Allen Dr.
Charlottesville, VA 22903
(888) 970-JUNK

This service contacts telemarketers and tells them to place you on their "don't call" list. Also attempts to limit unsolicited email (not an easy task). Ask for current fees.

Private Citizen, Inc.
Box 233
Naperville, IL 60566
(800) CUT-JUNK
Contacts eight largest direct mail firms and asks them to take you off their lists (also fee based).

Junkbusters
www.junkbusters.com
See their web site for free services to help you reduce both snail mail and email solicitations.

You can learn more about the direct mail industry by writing for a free brochure from:

Direct Marketing Association
1120 Avenue of the Americas
New York, NY 10036
A 20-page booklet called "Stop Junk Mail Forever" is available for $3.00 from:

Good Advise Press
PO Box 78
Elizaville, NY 12533
(800) 255-0899

In general, you should never purchase anything advertised through email or unsolicited snail mail as you will just make matters worse. Contacting the company that sent you the solicitation is often not a solution either because they won't necessarily take your name off their list and it will just confirm your present location.

Financial transactions

All of your checks, credit card transactions and wire transfers are recorded. If the account is in your name, the paper trail belongs to you. The only way you can stop this is to use accounts that do not have your name attached to them. This means bank accounts, credit cards, debit cards, and any type of investment. You can keep your present identity if you use trusts and this may be the best solution. Establishing a new identity and being consistent is a big hassle. Unless you're running from the law or trying to avoid a stalker (or the Mafia), just using trusts is the easiest and cleanest way to disassociate yourself from financial transactions you'd like to keep private.

Don't provide driver's license number or other personal information to retailers except what's printed on the checks. You may *show* them a driver's license for identification, but don't let them write down it's number. If they insist, shop elsewhere. Don't provide *any* personal information when using a credit card. Don't ever give out credit card numbers or other personal information on the phone unless you are sure about the company and have initiated the call.

You can get W-8 bank accounts in your name without a Social Security Number or open them up in the name of a trust without a taxpayer identification number, but discretion is advised. If a person opens up an account and does not follow directions explicitly, they may come under the scrutiny of bank officials (and the IRS or Revenue Canada). All U.S. banks now report to the IRS on all "interest bearing" W-8 accounts, so if a person accidentally opened up a W-8 account that was "interest bearing" instead of "non-interest bearing", then details would be reported to the IRS. It is not a good idea however, to trust that your bank is going to follow procedures and only report what they are supposed to report. There is a reward for turning in tax evaders. A U.S. address connected to the account also allows the paper trail to lead to a foreign trust. Canadian citizens should also be aware of these issues, because treaties between the two countries allow for sharing of information between Revenue Canada and the U.S. government. You might want to consider the use of a "demand deposit" account in a foreign or private onshore bank. This gives you the ability to transfer assets, especially cash, completely privately and they usually pay a reasonable annual return. I'm not advocating here that you evade lawful taxes on activity that is constitutionally taxable, but you need to know that there are ways of using banks privately to conduct your affairs. The problem with banks is that they might report an account or activity which is perfectly legal as being "suspicious" and then you have to deal with the bureaucracy (probably losing access to those assets while you straighten things out).

See the section on resources for information about trusts. The combination of a trust and an account with a "private" bank, especially one off-shore, is a very effective way of keeping your business dealings and/or assets secret. You will ideally want to have more than one trust, putting assets that have no possibility of creating a liability in one and assets like planes, boats, and automobiles that can be involved in accidents where someone might want to sue, into others. This way even if someone sues the boat trust for a million dollars and is successful, they can't touch any of your other assets. You can also have a business trust set up for your business assets. This separates that entity from all others. Trusts are not expensive to set up or administer and are extremely effective in stopping judgments, liens, lawsuits, levies, and other kinds of threats from stealing your assets. They are also very effective in keeping the IRS and other government agencies out of your business. Even the Chief of Accounting for the IRS has announced that "A Pure Trust Organization has no tax requirements." Therefore there is no legal requirement for it to even file a tax return. Be sure you use competent advisors to set up a trust so that all pertinent laws are followed in the countries involved. Don't buy a ready-made one that only requires that you fill in the spaces. Laws change constantly and you need to work with people who will keep up with the latest developments in contract law and taxation. Look in the resources section for organizations that can provide help with trusts.

You should also look into setting up a charitable foundation as part of your trust structure. These have been found to be very useful tool for avoiding fishing expeditions by government agencies and also enable you to actually do some valuable charitable work.

A contract in the form of a Pure Trust Organization (PTO) does not owe it's existence to any act of the legislature. It is created under the authority of the common-law right of parties to enter into a contract. As such, according to the Constitution of the United States, Article 1, § 10, the government cannot infringe upon this right to contract in any way. Even a judge cannot change any part of such a contract. Once property is transferred into a Pure Trust Organization, it is subject only to it's own indentures. The government can only regulate and tax entities which it creates or allows to exist as privileges. Since the contract is considered a right and not a privilege, the government has no claims or authority over it. Therefore, it is very effective for tax purposes. Revocable Living Trusts, Limited Liability Companies, and Corporations derive from statues that allow their existence and are therefore subject to legislative authority and may be regulated and taxed. They are exercising the privilege of operating as granted by the state in which they exist and are therefore subject to regulation and taxation. For this reason, Living Trusts, so commonly solicited these days are worth very little when it comes to really protecting your assets.

Because PTO's are a separate entity in themselves, they can also be used, along with a bank account in their name, for successfully transacting business. This separates you from the transactions and therefore from the paper trail. This is especially nice because the PTO also does not have a Social Security Number or Taxpayer Identification Number, since it is not a taxable entity. Now it is perfectly legal for you to pledge your services to a trust and you may also benefit from activities that the trust performs. For instance, you might have to withdraw cash acquired with a private bank VISA/debit card through an ATM machine for expenses required to conduct the business of the trust. The trust might wish to purchase property or automobiles that you are allowed to live in, drive, or use in any manner for which you see fit. It is important that you do not co-mingle funds however. You will always want to keep your own personal funds and those of the trust separate. You cannot pass property back and forth between yourself and the trust or have trust funds deposited directly into your personal bank account. You will get in trouble and the link will be passed on to credit bureaus, the IRS, and other agencies, public and private, if you do so. Any significant assets should be purchased by the trust. This is not to say that the trust cannot buy, sell, or transfer property, it can, just like any other form of business, but the "Trust Estate" is irrevocable, and therefore an unscrupulous creditor can't take you to court to try to force you to revoke the trust and free up your property so he can attach it! In general, you can effectively use trusts to conduct your affairs, just follow the law and use experts who are keeping up with it so that if any changes need to be made, you can do so in expeditiously.

The IRS has begun to examine trusts very closely and has trained some 1000 employees to audit trusts. One thing they look for is recently transferred assets. If you do a wire transfer of over $10,000, it will be reported to the IRS by the bank. If you transfer physical assets like cars, boats, or art work, they will try to follow the paper trail to the new owner (the trust). Even when the trust is in another country, they may try to intimidate the trust officials in that country. They also like to claim that if any assets were transferred in the two year span prior to the time in question, then it was done as a sham or a fraud.

If you file a tax return, you are supposed to reveal if you have any foreign bank accounts, securities, or trusts. If you lie on the return, you may be liable for penalties. Assuming you file the return and tell the truth, you must also file form 3520, naming the trustee and the beneficiaries, in the year you set up the trust and in every year in which you make a transfer to, or receive a distribution from, the trust. If your accounts contain over $10,000, you are also supposed to file a form TDF-90 showing account numbers and balances. If the beneficiaries are

Americans, such as you and your relatives, you are also supposed to file form 3520-A revealing Social Security Number's, rights to income, an income statement, and balance sheet for the trusts.

The IRS claims that, for U.S. citizens, earnings on foreign accounts, including brokerage accounts, are taxable. The IRS may file criminal charges with the Justice Department or levy penalties of 35% of the value of the property transferred on people who open foreign accounts and fail to file the correct forms. A foreign trust can however make all the money it wants and never report to anyone. If you work for a trust or are an administrator, you don't own it, and you also don't own it's assets or any of the profits from any businesses it may run. The whole idea here is that you don't own a trust, it's not your trust. It is a contract between parties. You may be merely an employee or agent of a trust that was set up somewhere by someone (not yourself)! You don't have any accounts, earnings, property, securities, distributions, or anything else in a foreign country, a trust does! Therefore you don't have any filing or reporting requirements as "you" haven't conducted any taxable or reportable activities! Now are you catching on? Be sure to follow the directions for proper interaction with any trust and you will protect yourself from unscrupulous others with plans for your hard earned money.

How would the IRS find out about such foreign accounts or trusts? People are sloppy. They transfer over $10,000 from a domestic bank in their name who reports it, they tell friends or relatives what they're doing, an ex-spouse, a neighbor, or a fellow employee reports them just to do his patriotic duty. The IRS pays a 10% reward up to $100,000, to people who report tax "evaders". You don't want to be labeled a tax evader if you aren't one! Remember, you don't own a trust! Don't tell people you "have a trust" as they will certainly misunderstand.

It is fairly easy to follow a paper trail of transferred assets. Private Investigators do this all the time. If there's any weakness in the trust structure, they will find it. That is why you want to use reliable private banks, preferably in foreign countries with good reputations for secrecy. It is perfectly legal to sell your house to another person or entity. You can legally sell it to a trust! This is not unusual. You can also quitclaim it over to a trust entity. Businesses buy and sell property between various "entities" all the time. You just want to use care in the way you liquidate any assets. They could be sold to a non-involved third party and that party could sell or transfer it into a trust. Assets could be sold for cash and later the cash used to purchase new things by an entity which then lets you use them, or requires you to use them in the course of your employment as an agent. Don't be intimidated, especially when you're acting completely within the law. Remember that the rich and powerful (including politicians) have been using these strategies for years.

1. If you'd like to truly leave the system and stop playing the bank/credit/government game, close all bank accounts and credit cards associated with your name.
2. Use a foreign VISA/debit card established for an entity and without your name on it (see resources section).
3. Pay cash whenever possible for all purchases, but don't make *large* purchases with cash, instead use a VISA/MC owned by an entity. The entity should make any large purchases with a wire transfer. Remember, don't own anything of significant value.
4. You can try to open up a bank account without a Social Security Number if you need a local bank, but keep in mind that many banks will report even W-8 interest bearing *or* non-interest bearing accounts to government agencies (use only for few, small unimportant transactions if you must have a local bank account).
5. People have been known to purchase International Driver's Permits in an alias name and use them to open domestic bank accounts, thereby not having to divulge any Social Security/Insurance Numbers.
6. All credit transactions should be thought of with one thing in mind: they establish a paper trail. Make sure that this paper trail supports your new "official" identity. You, as an

individual, make very little money, and work for a company that engages in normal business activities.

7. Remember that many offshore banks *will* exchange information with U.S. government agencies, if asked.
8. The newly printed federal reserve notes and Canadian currency have built-in features that can identify them. It is possible that if you gave a bank your Social Security/Insurance Number when withdrawing a large amount, they could be run through a reader and linked to you. The new bills may also be traceable by machines that can penetrate your wallet or pocketbook and determine the existence of the bill even at a distance of several feet. The government is always looking for possible money laundering. Don't deal in large amounts of cash, especially for airline tickets. Instead use a private bank and a credit/debit card established in the name of a trust or wire money if necessary.
9. The Cayman Islands recently signed an agreement with the U.S. to report "any suspicious activity". Many other countries have these agreements with the U.S. government too, supposedly to fight the drug trade. There are only a few countries that offer complete privacy. Try not to do business in a country that has signed these agreements with the U.S. See the reference section on private and not so private countries.
10. Under U.S. law it is illegal to transfer (or move out of the country) more than $10,000 without reporting it to the IRS. Don't transfer large amounts of money in your name. Use trusts and wire transfers.
11. Money laundering is now defined in over 150 different ways. There are even bounty hunters who get paid to report you. Be discreet. Your bank teller can receive a reward for reporting "suspicious activity". Don't be suspicious. Don't use local banks if at all possible.
12. Pay bills by cash or money order rather than by cashier's check as the banks always want a remitter's name. Large

transactions should be via wire transfer between a trust and the payee.

Purchases

International banks and multinational corporations seeking ever more power are insatiable. Smart cards are already in widespread use in Europe and some Asian countries. Bull Smart Cards claims to have over 120 million in use around the world. These devices are about the size of credit cards and have embedded chips that hold various types of information or cash value. They are touted as offering convenience and security because the encryption is tougher to crack than the magnetic stripe on most current credit cards and they effectively prevent payment fraud and counterfeit money. They are particularly popular in France, where they started out as prepaid phone cards. Today, in Singapore, the CashCard acts as electronic money for movies, parking, gas and fast food restaurants. Smart cards have been used in banking, healthcare, transportation, tollbooths, and vending machines. The heads of VISA, MasterCard, and American Express among others are moving ahead with implementing the cashless society where *everything* is purchased with a type of smart card. Guess who's in control of your purchase decisions when they are in charge of the Smart Cards? Imagine the following scenario: "I'm sorry ma'am, your card is invalid. No we don't take cash, only The Card." You can only purchase goods and services where and when someone else dictates. If cash is not an option, you're stuck, even if the information preventing you from purchasing is false or implanted by someone with whom you disagree (or a hacker). Could you go without food, medical care, shelter, and other necessities for a year or longer while you try to get things straightened out? Are you willing to be at the mercy of unknown bureaucrats or corporate clerks who can dictate your every transaction?

Smart cards are becoming more widespread and can even be read while still in your pocket or purse, from a distance of as much as 100 feet. On the other hand, even though banks trust the smart card technology, the security has already been broken over 4 years ago. It has only recently been reported in the *New York Times* that a gentleman named Paul Kocher has been able to independently break the codes and has revealed his knowledge to the producers in hopes that they might be able to come up with a way of strengthening the cards before crooks also discovered how to crack them. The technology used in the cards is becoming fairly widely known and it is even possible to purchase a card holder, or sleeve to prevent access to the data on the cards without the owners knowledge. The special holder is made from a material that blocks out the low frequency magnetic field used to read the contents. You might want to check out www.megsinet.com/jeffp/ for more information on this product (available for about $30.00).

Of course, your purchases, made with a regular credit card or one of these smart cards that can hold digital cash, also provide a paper trail of your activities and whereabouts. All of these details can be obtained by someone who may want to know what you're doing. All they have to do is to call up the credit card company and impersonate you. They'll have to gather some personal information about you first, but as you have already read, this is not difficult. They then claim that "you" lost your card and want a list of all recent purchases (plus locations). After the person gives out all of the pertinent information, the impersonator abruptly says "Oh, here it is, I found it in a drawer, thank-you very much."

Here is a list of things you can do to protect yourself at retail establishments when engaging in any kind of financial transaction:

1. Don't let sales clerks write down your driver's license number on credit card purchases (or give them any identifying information). You can show it to them, but don't physically hand it over to them. Use money orders, cash, and your private P.O. box when you make purchases by mail order (remember to request that your name not be shared or sold).

2. Don't write checks at Radio Shack or other stores that computerize your address and phone number.
3. Use cash for all purchases if possible. Alternately you can use money orders or a VISA/debit card from a private bank see resources section on private banks). Be careful about who you do business with if you use any kind of credit card.
4. Ask the retail stores you patronize not to give out personal information about you without some confirmation that the person asking is truly you. Do this with the phone company, utilities, cable companies, and delivery services too.

Credit card companies and credit bureaus

Credit cards

Visa, Master Card, Discover, and American Express cards (among others) are in extremely wide use, especially on the Internet. American Express revealed in May of 1998 that it regularly sells its mailing list to marketing companies. It also makes available a great deal of other information about its card holders, like their buying habits and places they visit. Representatives from Visa and Master Card have also said that your information is available from the companies that use them even if they don't sell your name directly. You can request that your credit card companies not distribute your name. Look for forms that come with new cards where you can specify that you don't want your name distributed or call their 800 numbers.

If someone wants to gather information about you, credit card companies and credit bureaus are one of their biggest bargains as they pride themselves in knowing everything about you (and your spouse). If you want to appear "normal" you should have 3-4 credit cards. Credit bureaus offer many services including turning a Social Security Number into a name and address, telephone and address directories, name searches, employment histories, and even driving records.

Other than the federal government, nobody has more information on you than the credit bureaus. Your records are also coded. 01's indicating you pay on time and 03's and 09's showing charge-offs. If someone without your best interests in mind wants your credit records, they can get them even though you may be told that even private investigator's don't have access to them. One bureau, CBI is itself a P.I. agency. You just have to have a "legitimate reason", like having your own business, to gain access. Some private investigator's open up sham businesses to present the illusion of legitimacy. Another way is illegal, but used: the person gets the dial up number and subscriber code for a bureau. Obtaining the dial up number is relatively easy by impersonating an employee of a large bank and telling the bureau that you're filling in for the person who usually runs the credit bureaus but who is sick and you need help. They may even tell you the number and give complete instructions on how to run a credit report. Banks and most businesses are so lax that you can even call a large bank and claim to be from another branch, then ask them for the dial up number. Small businesses often have the number and the subscriber code tacked up on their computer screens so a call claiming to be from one of the bureaus and saying you want to confirm they're using the right subscriber code will often result in the person giving out that information.

Don't ever believe that businesses in general or financial institutions in particular are careful with your records. Dumpster diving is even a highly effective way to gather lots of credit reports. For those people who are really lazy, they can pay someone $75.00 to run a credit report (which only costs $2.00). There is really no way to remove your name from their records. The only thing you can do is to stop the bleeding. Don't use your name in any more financial transactions. If you can't pay with cash, use a private or off-shore VISA/debit card in the name of a trust. All major purchases should be done in the name of a trust. Just stop using your own name. If you wish to establish a new identity, you have a perfect right to do so, but it's not completely necessary unless you're being stalked or harassed.

See the section at the end on resources if you want more information about identities.

Credit bureaus

The three main credit reporting agencies generally don't disclose specific information about the names of your creditors and amounts owed when they sell your name to marketing companies. They do however, make available customized lists of people with particular characteristics, like those falling in various income categories or who use credit cards regularly and pay their bills on time. They will provide details to companies that request it for credit granting purposes. You can call or write to the bureaus and ask that your name be removed from the lists they sell for credit pre-screening purposes. Recent legislation related to the Fair Credit Reporting Act requires that they allow this. It's always better to write a letter and include your signature (keep a copy for yourself).

To request that your name not be sold:

Equifax Options
Equifax Marketing Decision Systems, Inc.
P.O. Box 740123
Atlanta, GA 30374
(800) 556-4711

To check on your own records:

Equifax, Inc.
PO Box 740241
Atlanta, GA 30374-0241
(800) 685-1111

To request that your name not be sold:

Experian (formerly TRW)
Target Marketing Services Division
Attn. Consumer Opt Out
P.O. Box 919

Allen, TX 75013
(800) 353-0809

To check on your own records:

Experian
National Consumer Relations Center
PO Box 749028
Dallas, TX 75374-9029
1 (800) 682-7654

To request that your name not be sold:

Transunion
Name Removal Option
P.O. Box 97328
Jackson, MS 39288-7328

To check on your own records:

Transunion Corp.
Customer Relations Dept.
PO Box 7000, 25249 Country Club Blvd.
North Olmstead, OH 44070
1 (216) 779-7200

Additional information regarding your current known credit report:

Associated Credit Services/CSC Credit Services, Inc.
652 N. Belt East
Houston, TX 77060
1 (713) 878-1900 or 1 (800) 759-5979

If you *do* contact any of the above, remember, don't volunteer any personal information that is absolutely not required and don't send them a personal check for their services. All kinds of information is available on checks. See the section on strategies for a suggested overall strategy in dealing with credit. You may decide that you don't want to have anything to do with the above agencies and writing them may be unnecessary.

Banking and investing

Banks are very interesting institutions. They have but one purpose in their existence and that is to make as much money as possible. How is this different from any other business? Well, banks have a distinct advantage. They can make money from your money and they can also make it out of nothing! Since they can take in $100.00 and loan out $1000.00 (according to Federal Reserve rules which require a 10% reserve on deposits over about $50 million, but only 3% under that) , they essentially have the ability to loan out more than they take in. In other words, they can loan out money that they don't have! This in essence creates money. It would be like you opening up a shoe store and selling shoes that you don't have. You would issue a little IOU note that says the customer will get the shoes when someone else comes back to the store and returns shoes they bought already. But of course customers have to pay for the shoes right away, or at least pay a monthly fee for access to them. Banks make a lot of their money on fees they attach to every kind of transaction. They take in $100.00 and then loan out $900.00, making a hefty fee on the $900 and paying a tiny interest rate to the $100.00. Because they have so much imaginary money to play with, they can offer a wide range of services, all for a fee of course. What they really want is to have a piece of every transaction that is ever made between anyone or any entity anywhere. Cash is really a nuisance to them and they'd rather just do everything electronically. They are currently establishing vast systems for "wealth cards" that can be used for every type of transaction, including normal purchases, medical payments and records, and investing. These cards would contain everything about you from cradle to grave and would do everything that could be done with money or in any kind of transaction you could possibly have with another person or business.

Now banks are always complaining about being over-regulated. They really think they know better than anyone else what is best for the money supply and the economy. They have some very powerful people who support them too. Fed Chairman Alan Greenspan, for one, has abandoned the notion that it is possible to regulate this broad frontier with old-style rules. The burden, he says, has to rest with private industry to regulate themselves. "To continue to be effective, government's regulatory role must increasingly assure that effective risk-management systems are in place in the private sector," he observed in a 1996 paper. "As financial systems become more complex, detailed rules and standards have become both burdensome and ineffective." In fact, many governments are competing with one another to see who can offer the fewest regulations. And the money is following right along. Economist Skoorka calls this regulatory arbitrage, the flight of money from highly regulated markets to barely regulated ones. And as these superbanks battle to survive against the Microsofts of the world, a battle in which the outcome is still anything but certain, we all become more like numbers and less like humans.

Consumers might find this terrifying, but the superbankers love it. Because the gigantic banks are too large to fail, firms like the new BankAmerica and Citigroup are touted as offering the safest possible havens for investors, safer, perhaps, than even government-printed money. In the end, what the financiers are after is not just new customers or new deposits, but a kind of business immortality ensured by their gargantuan size and guaranteed by their technology. E-cash, wealth accounts and consumer derivatives will have made these firms as essential as cash itself once was. If business immortality can be purchased, these are the people who will figure out how to finance it. And they will be doing so with your money. Keep in mind that your privacy is of no concern to them, you are a number and a source of income. Actually, they prefer that you have <u>no</u> access to secrecy, while on the other hand, they jealously guard their own.

Those wonderfully convenient ATM machines take your picture every time you use them. Your name and account number is recorded along with the details of the transaction (including date, time, and location). If you do not wish to be identified, you'll have to wear sunglasses or some other form of concealing garment like a hat or even false facial hair. Some banks are requiring thumb prints even to use an ATM card and computers are becoming so sophisticated that they can take digital pictures of your face or hand for identification purposes. You can prevent ATM transactions from recording your name by using a debit card that doesn't have your name encoded on it. See the section on materials available for regaining and protecting your personal and financial privacy at the end of this manual for debit cards you can obtain which have only the name of a trust or other entity electronically recorded and reveal nothing about your personal identity. These can be obtained at very reasonable cost and are well worth the price. These cards often come with unlimited withdrawal capabilities too as an added benefit. You can place money into the account anonymously and use the card for cash any time and anywhere you wish. They are usually a VISA or Master Card and therefore very versatile for purchases as well as obtaining cash.

The elderly especially need to protect their savings and resources. They are the frequent target of scams and con artists. The least they should do is to get an unlisted phone number and then never believe telemarketers or strangers on the phone with information or prizes to give away. They should never give out any personal information on the phone to people who have called them unless they positively know the person. Their names are passed around and sold to scam artists of all kinds. Some crooks even make it a point to watch the obituaries, looking for rich widows they can make friends with, by attending the same church, or calling them and claiming to be a long lost friend of the deceased, etc. Next thing you know, the poor woman is sending them money. Widows should always get unlisted numbers right away after the death of their husbands, if they don't have one already. They also need to be especially vigilant, by not giving out the number to anyone except closest friends and relatives. If a business wants it, they should refuse if at all possible and if they must give it out, they must specify that it is not to be given out to anyone, for any reason! They should also never have their unlisted phone number on their checks. For that matter, I don't recommend that anyone put their phone numbers on checks. Additionally, all of their major assets should be owned by a trust. If the widow's assets are in a trust and she only has a limited amount of money in a local checking or savings account, she is not so likely to be a target. Crooks, including large institutions, look for assets and the ability of a person to take on debt. They want your money, or a lien on your house.

Banks will also give out information about your recent checks in addition to your balance if you claim to have lost your check book. Even Swiss banks can be tricked into confirming that you have an account with them. If someone has your date of birth and passport number as identifying information, a bank representative can be tricked into revealing your account by the person claiming to be the account holder and saying that their ex-spouse is trying to get at their money and you want to be sure they haven't been successful. If your name is attached to an account, the details of the account are available to anyone. A very effective way of getting access to someone's bank records is to file a $31.00 lawsuit against them and subpoena the records.

Subpoenas are issued without question by the county clerks office. The only way you can protect yourself and your financial information is to have it with banks and other financial institutions in another name or trust known only to yourself!

In reference to the so called "Bank Secrecy Act" of 1970, you need to know that all_of your bank records are available to the government, especially the IRS. The IRS may issue a summons to a bank and get access to everything dating back to the time you opened your account, and including any notes written by any bank employees about you! These notes may be pure conjecture about your behavior or motives for any transactions you've had with the bank. You can file a motion to stop such a summons in a federal district court, but you won't win. Even W-8 non-interest bearing accounts that can be opened without Social Security Numbers are not recommended anymore because of the pressure the government is putting on the banks to reveal any possible unusual dealings or transactions.

It's become fairly easy to find out everything about someone's bank account these days even if you don't work for the IRS. If someone has your account number it's even easier, so you should not have your new blank checks delivered to an unlockable mail box. Aside from obvious thieves, fully legitimate companies come to the rescue of strangers who would like to know everything about your bank records. A story in the June 11, 1998 issue of the *Washington Post* states that your bank records can be purchased by anyone through data brokers:

The story explains how companies like Advanced Research Inc. in Stroudsburg, Pa., advertise their ability to deliver details about account balances, stock portfolios and many other assets. TR Information Services in Miami says they can take orders 24 hours a day. The Pathfinder Group in Falls Church claims it can deliver its financial reports in four days or less. Their $325 Enhanced Bank Account Search can provide minute details of bank transactions and up-to-the-minute account balances. These information brokers pose as customers and keep asking for information until they find someone who will give them the information they want. They make use of widely available personal information, such as a Social Security Numbers, to get more details, using pretexts like they can't find their checkbooks or their wife has it. These searches range in cost from just over $100 for a modest search to several thousand dollars for a nationwide accounting of bank accounts, stocks, mutual funds, and safety deposit boxes. The president of TR Information Services, Todd Mayers, has admitted that he is not sure how all his subcontractors get the information sold by his firm. Michael Martin, president of Advanced Research, admits his company uses pretext calling.

There has been some backlash however. Officials in Massachusetts announced fines against four companies that secretly obtained financial information about Massachusetts residents. Search firms in Massachusetts, California, Missouri and Washington were fined $60,000 in civil penalties and barred from that practice in Massachusetts. An investigation was started after a bank security official in Boston saw an ad for one of the information services and anonymously ordered a search on himself. Later officials said the methods used by the services were a violation of consumer protection laws prohibiting unfair or deceptive business practices. There is also some interest in Congress. Rep. Jim Leach (R-Iowa), chairman of the House Banking Committee, reportedly is looking into the sale of financial information. Furthermore, law enforcement authorities have said that brokers who misrepresent themselves might be breaking state laws prohibiting the release of confidential data without a customer's permission. A Justice Department spokesman said callers obtaining information by posing as a customer might also be violating federal wire fraud laws. The information services industry is very large however, so don't expect them to accept limitations without a fight. An official from the American Bankers Association, says the problems with information brokers can be solved through existing policies and procedures, not legislation that would put pressure on them to strengthen their procedures.

The bottom line is, don't trust your bank. Any information or records about you in your bank can belong to anyone. Pick a private bank that uses codes, pass phrases and other security measures to validate ALL calls for information. Open up a trust account, and don't put <u>any</u> personal information in the records. Even safety deposit boxes are not private if they are in your name. Safety deposit boxes can actually be a serious problem if you die and the box is sealed (or if it's broken into). You should follow these rules when choosing a bank for private financial dealings:

1. Don't pick a bank with any branches in the U.S.
2. Choose a bank where English is the primary language.
3. Choose one that offers credit cards, like VISA/MC.
4. Don't use a bank that makes you fill out a form releasing information to the U.S. or Canadian government.
5. Try to use one that offers a dollar denominated checkbook.
6. Use a bank that can also offer trusts or will honor trusts.
7. Don't bank where they allow phone-in computer access using Social Security/Insurance Numbers as passwords. Better yet, don't bank at any local bank, except for very minor check writing purposes for small items. Use an international bank in a country that will respect your privacy.

If you want to hide money and not involve a bank, you can use savings bonds, money orders or travelers checks.

Insurance

Controlling who has access to your medical and insurance files is difficult, but some things can be done. You may need to be able to make corrections and add statements to your records if you feel that there are inaccuracies, so you might want to check your records once a year with your local health provider (including dentist) and with the Medical Insurance Bureau mentioned earlier. You can do without insurance, especially liability and errors and omissions, if all of your major assets are in trusts (no one can sue you). If you have a business, be sure to discuss your concerns with a competent attorney who is very familiar with pure trusts in order to satisfy yourself that you are protected. If you want life insurance to provide money to your family in the case of your demise, you are going to be subjected to the usual questions about your health history and have to give them a Social Security Number. If you'd like to purchase health insurance without a Social Security

Number, call your local NASE representative at (800) 232-NASE (National Association for the Self Employed) or at www.nase.org.

There is also an organization called Conquest. They pride themselves in helping you with your health care planning with complete privacy. You can also self-insure by putting away money for emergencies and then pay cash for medical care, giving the provider no identifying information, or using an alternate identity. If the medical ID number legislation is allowed to become law, we may all soon lose the right of private medical care. What would you tell your doctor if you knew that everything you said would become part of a huge dossier on you available to just about anyone else. Oh, did I mention the possibilities of errors in your file - you can count on errors, inaccuracies, omissions, hearsay, opinions, conclusions, deductions, incomplete documentation or lack of explanations for important data. After almost 20 years in the database field, I guarantee there will be errors in your file! You might consider getting prescriptions filled and medical care outside the country. You'll even save money.

Travel

Traveling outside the country can get you on a watch list. FinCEN, mentioned earlier, looks for the following in determining whether you merit further investigation:

- Travel outside the country more than four times per year, especially to the Caribbean or South America.
- Three or more CTR's over $3000.00 per year.
- Real estate holdings over $200,000.
- Officer or director of more than 10 corporations.

Here are some important things to remember when traveling, whether it domestic or internationally:

1. If you need to travel outside the country, buy a ticket (using a corporate credit card) to a place like Mexico City. Then purchase a new ticket with a different credit card (corporate or in a different name) to the actual destination. On the return trip, come back through Mexico City.
2. At the airport, if you hear the warning announcement regarding the need to report carrying $10,000 in cash outside of the country, they're probably suspecting someone and need to have the announcement aired, so be careful. When you stay at a hotel, see if they will take a cash deposit instead of a credit card for potential room charges.
3. Never make calls from your hotel room phone, except down to the front desk or for room service.
4. Always use public phones elsewhere for important calls. Use phone cards for these calls. They are available just about everywhere, but you'll probably want to get them in the country you're calling from to make sure they work in that locality.
5. Avoid traveling outside the country more than four times a year, especially to the Caribbean, unless you have a very conventional reason for doing so. This avoids the government fishing expeditions looking for drug dealers and money launderers.

Taxes

Everyone who has ever filed a tax return in the U.S. has what is called an Individual Master File. This file serves as a basis for your "Non-Master" file which is not accessible by the public. A Business Master File is also attached to the IMF in many cases. If an agent makes up fictitious codes making you responsible for taxes you don't even know about, you may be placed into a whole new category. Now, as a backup withholding agent for the IRS, you are required to file a 1040 form. If you go ahead and sign one, you are admitting to being a "taxpayer" and surrender all of your rights. If you go to court, it will undoubtedly be in a "tax court" where the only thing a judge wants to hear is how much in taxes do you owe? Naturally the IRS will say that you are liable and you won't even be able to argue that issue at all. You may even be liable for new taxes and penalties that would never applied to you as an individual, but now do as a business. These can increase a tax bill of a couple thousand dollars to hundreds of thousands overnight.

If you suspect that your IMF is incorrect because of some unpleasant experience with the IRS, and you wish to dispute it, you can get access to it, but you'll need help decoding all of the hieroglyphics. For example, as a result of an unfriendly meeting with a tax auditor or other official, your records may be labeled with TC 148, the code for "illegal tax protestor". There is no code for "legal" tax protestor as far as we have been able to find. It doesn't take much to be labeled as an illegal tax protester. You simply ask the IRS for a copy of your files in order to find out what your public servants at the IRS are up to and the IRS will label you as an illegal tax protester. A company called Trask Products, has specialized in examining these files and can help people who have been subjected to IRS investigations or allegations. They are often able to not only refute the charges against the citizen, but also provide evidence of felony mail and computer fraud against the agents involved. They have found that when a thorough examination of the files is completed and a strong defense developed, the IRS always backs down and refuses to go to court, where the truth might come out for the public to hear and expose them to embarrassment, plus the potential of millions in damages. Of course, you can "win" against the government and still lose! A defense can cost you thousands of dollars and if you don't get to take them to court and sue them for the costs (plus more hopefully in damages), you just spent all of your money and the government spent the taxpayers'. See the resources section for how to get in touch with Trask Products.

Having a Social Security/Insurance Number is totally voluntary for most citizens, even though you are asked for it whenever you attempt to do just about anything of a financial nature in the U.S. and Canada. Probably most of our representatives are not even aware of the voluntary nature of the Social Security System. What most people do not understand is that there really is no Social Security "Trust Fund" either in the U.S. or Canada. ALL of your social security contributions are treated as a tax and go into the general fund! There are absolutely no restrictions on their use by the federal government and basically these funds have been completely spent through the years. It is really the world's biggest Ponzi scheme, whereby future payouts are funded by the contributions of new or current people in the system. Nothing is really saved for the future. If however, you have one of these cards and you are receiving benefits from the government, you are liable for payment for the benefits you receive. You do not have to have or use one of these cards! It is possible to live in this country without one, though there are many inconveniences and challenges to face (and the situation is getting worse).

If you wish to learn more about the Constitution and your rights with regard to taxes, you need to avail yourself of the many books and reference materials available which are listed in the reference section. Pay special attention to the author's arguments and their win-loss record with the courts. It matters not if you are 100% right if you lose in court! Beware of authors who ask you to contribute to the legal costs of those they have defended and for which they lost the cases! You can win and you can maintain your freedoms and your rights, but you must choose leaders who have the experience and the ability to carry you through to victory! There is no substitute for doing your own homework and familiarizing yourself with the issues at hand. There are organizations with excellent track records, which have been helping and educating people for many years. See the resource section at the end of this book.

The opinion of the author is that the so-called "income tax" has, as its primary purpose, the control of American citizens by controlling their finances. If the government knows all about your financial affairs, it can dictate what you can and cannot do, what you can buy, how you can invest, where you put your money, whether you save or not, and how much you can earn. There are many Constitutionally lawful means of raising money for government purposes. Taxes could be levied against businesses or business activities, against purchases, against ownership of property, or many other things. It is totally unnecessary for the government to ask Americans to annually divulge every detail of their financial affairs and then assess a tax against those "activities" or assets. The government just wants to know your business! They can then run all kinds of programs or make innumerable changes to the financial or social fabric of the country by playing with "deductions" or "exemptions". Individuals and business make decisions every day that depend wholly or in part on the effect on their tax bill rather than on what is financially or productively prudent! The government coerces the populace into behaviors it wants by making threats of tax penalties or even jail. You have to decide if you want continue to give the government this much control over your life. Remember though, that the government plays hard ball and doesn't always play by the rules (or it interprets the rules to benefit itself). Government bureaucrats want to keep their jobs and maintaining the status quo is one way of doing that. Keep in mind also that administrations and members of Congress come and go, but the Constitution remains constant. Always go back to that, get to know it, and use it to keep yourself free.

Possessions

1. Diversify your assets and include some in offshore investments.
2. Don't buy gold in the U.S. or keep it in the U.S. Buy and keep it offshore. Many say also that gold in the form of

bullion or dollars is a poor investment. They recommend only rare gold or silver coins which are worth more than their face value or their weight melted down. At times the U.S. government has also confiscated gold in various forms, except for rare coins owned by "collectors" (you must always call yourself a collector of rare coins).

3. Don't own an airplane, boat, car, or other large asset in your name. See section on trusts for all important assets including your house).
4. Make sure you have your assets in trusts for your family so there's no problem with the transition when you die. Give away everything not in a trust.
5. Use a trust to purchase a house or use another person to buy it and let you rent or lease (remember rule about not owning anything).

Licenses

Renewing licenses can be a problem if you are a professional like a CPA or have a pilots license for example. One way private investigators and bounty hunters find someone with a pilot's license is to find out when their next physical is due and where and then show up there with papers to serve or handcuffs. Even if you wish to renew a driver's license, states are being pressured by the federal government to require Social Security Numbers and sometimes even fingerprints to get or renew a license. You may want to consider getting a drivers license in a state that doesn't require Social Security Numbers or using an international driver's license (see resources section). If you drive a car owned by a trust, you can say that it is a company car, and indeed it is! You can therefore have a driver's license in any state or an international license.

Your professional licenses are a link to your identity and financial activities. This is OK as long as you work for a company and reliably report your income. This, of course, will be whatever you decide it will be. A CPA could conceivably work for a company and make only $20,000 a year if there were other benefits. Your "official" identity may remain the same professionally, but change financially in a dramatic way, diminishing your exposure to audits, lawsuits, and greedy scam artists.

If you own a business

1. Use an out of state corporate filing company or have a trust own your company.
2. Don't incorporate in California (or your state of residence). Remember that a limited partnership is the most private form of business except for a trust.
3. Beware of corporate espionage, including that from your own government.
4. Check out all employees who have access to sensitive documents or information.
5. Keep a strict security policy in effect at all times. Get a professional company to do an inventory assessment and plan for you if you don't have in-house staff to do so.
6. Have your security regularly checked for weaknesses.
7. Don't give out keys to the offices except to those who absolutely need them. Re-key when a person leaves employment.
8. Don't allow strangers access to the corporate network in conference rooms.
9. Don't allow any computer media to enter or leave the building unless it is checked out.
10. Get control over your sensitive data by encrypting it and restricting access to the Internet, where viruses and trojan horse programs might cause all kinds of damage.

IV. Personal Safety and Privacy

Implanted chips and permanent ID's

Smart cards mentioned earlier, can hold a lot more than just cash value! They could hold information about any aspect of your life. The future is not just with smart cards though, it is in small implanted chips, the same as are already being sold to pet owners to find lost dogs and cats. An article in the *Wall Street Journal* Monday, April 20,1998 about electronic tags, radio frequency identification (RFID) discussed how this new technology is being used in wrist bracelets and is becoming very popular. The story discusses various new, "exciting" uses, including keeping track of children in temporary day care centers in stores, tracking Alzheimer's patients in nursing homes, controlling access to office buildings, and paying for purchases without cash. The bracelets or smart cards are also being used to track the location of employees and the use and location of equipment. The CEO of Sensormatic, Robert Vanourek wants retailers to start using RFID for customer tracking, giving customers cards that can track not only what they purchase, but where they go in the store and how much time they spend at each location. He assumes that customers will get used to the intrusion on their privacy, and he's probably right!

The article ends with a paragraph that asks the question: "While they're at it, why not implant ID tags in people?" The final paragraph does not contain one single sentence that acknowledges the dangers of this kind of monitoring; instead, it merely mentions Robert Vanourek's belief that "it will take time", but will eventually happen. He believes the earlobes will make the perfect location for such implants. It has been reported that some new parents in Canada have already been convinced to allow ID implants in the ears of their newborns in a supposed effort to prevent kidnapping. If this isn't Big Brother in action I don't know what is. There isn't much difference between a number on your wrist, like in Nazi Germany, and an electronic "tag" in your earlobe.

Public ID devices

You *pay* for convenience! The E-Z Pass sticker on your car that allows you to go through the tollbooth also records your location every time you pass through. You could pay cash. Other forms of identification include parking passes, school and business stickers for your car, and any other prepaid privileges where you are required to provide your name, address, phone, etc.

Demands for ID

Many stores ask for identifying information when you purchase something whether by cash, check, or credit card. Your should always refuse to provide anything and just say that you don't need any more junk mail. Resist their repeated requests and insistence that its only used for internal records and never shared. They lie. If you pay by check, they don't need anything more than what's already imprinted on the check, except for some form of identification. Try to avoid allowing them to record your driver's license number, but this may be required, and never give out your Social Security Number! If they need a credit card for ID, you can allow them to briefly look at it but you are not required to allow them to record the numbers and your shouldn't! If you can, pay with cash. Then you can't be asked for anything!

Surveillance

If someone hires a private investigator, they are going to do their homework beforehand. They will find out all they can about you first: your driving habits, patterns, hobbies, business locations and routines, places you frequent for business and pleasure, etc. They will try to build up a history on you, including where you go for lunch and any regular visits to health clubs, malls, stores, neighborhoods. They will try to get your phone records first (including the mobile phone) to try to find out who you call and where they live or work. These records are especially important because they also have a time which tells when you conduct your business or make connections to other important people. One of the private investigator's oldest tricks is to obtain the hotel telephone records of a person who goes out of town and feels invincible, but makes important calls from his hotel room. The pretext is fairly easy to pull off. Someone, usually a woman, is used to call the hotel and claim to be the subject's secretary or a member of the bookkeeping department and say they need the phone records to fill in the subject's expense report. Once phone records are obtained, addresses are easy to get using crisscross directories. Hotel room numbers can also be determined by claiming to be the subject. The investigator merely calls the front desk late at night claiming to be the subject and sounding a little drunk, then saying that he forgot his room number.

If you need added security because of a stalker, you may wish to rendezvous at malls or large department stores, especially at night. The latter are easy to watch and only take one person, but malls take two people, because there are many entrances and exits. One person must be in a car and the other on foot. If the surveillance team has a small budget, there will probably only be one person on it, so malls are a better choice (or large downtown department stores). If you want to lose a tail, head for congested traffic situations and watch for vehicles that are always just a couple cars behind you. Vans are often favored because the drivers are not as easy to spot. Also, women often are used for surveillance, especially the ones on foot, because, with a shopping bag, they look like thousands of others on the street.

You might be under surveillance from plain, ordinary voyeurs, who may also have the skills and equipment of a private investigator. They can buy the same cameras PI's can (that fit in smoke detectors or in a light switch) for under $300.00. If you rent a house or apartment, check it out first. Check every room. Look for unusual holes or objects that look out of place or askew. Check all smoke detectors, ventilation grates, places that could conceal a lens perhaps as small as a pencil eraser. If you rent a furnished apartment or house, you may want to also check the furniture. Check in the kitchen and bathroom. Look at the mirror in the bathroom. Turn off the light and then look at it again. Does it change color. Can you look behind it? Look in the ceiling fan (you can probably see a concealed lens with a flashlight and don't have to take the whole thing down). Even after doing an initial check, you should be aware of anything unusual. Only a professional TSCM sweep will find everything.

Any time you check into a hotel or motel, assume that it is wired for video and sound. Maybe it isn't, but assume it is. If you want privacy, you'll have to do your own check ... everyday. Look in all the same places as above and remember that furniture, TV's, radios, phones, and anything else electrical is a prime location for audio or video equipment. If you're only staying for the night and will be doing very boring, mundane things in your room, you don't have to be so careful, but if you're meeting someone in a situation that could be sensitive, take every precaution.

Assume that you are under video and maybe audio surveillance everywhere. All clothing stores have a legal excuse to record you in the dressing rooms. They may also have cameras in the rest rooms. You might be recorded in any public place, including sports facilities, public rest rooms, and all public, government buildings or properties. You see more and more stories of people using small camcorders strategically located in baggage, taping under women's skirts. You might want to be more aware of who is standing next to you in the bus, in line at the checkout counter, or in any crowded, public place. If you assume the worst, you will more likely avoid becoming a victim. Remember that video taping is not generally illegal. A recently passed anti-voyeur law in Washington State makes video taping a person illegal only if it's done purely for sexual gratification. It's difficult to prove that claim in court however, especially if the person has any way to say that it was for security purposes. You'll have to check the state you live in for laws relating to video and audio recordings. Chances are that only audio recording is prohibited unless both parties are informed but some states only require one party's consent. Don't count on the law protecting you , take care of yourself. Even if a person illegally records you and gets caught, your personal information or picture may appear on the Internet or elsewhere equally as embarrassing or threatening.

Mistakes you don't want to make

Most people have never thought about how to deal with this issue before and are unprepared for the sophistication of "the system", including government snoops, private investigators, and unwitting entities that participate in their loss of privacy. You need to start thinking about the implications for all your financial transactions. The list below includes common things people do to inadvertently advertise themselves and their activities, in effect sabotaging their own privacy.

1. Leaving a paper trail, especially in asset and money transfers. Don't assume that <u>any</u> business will protect your privacy.
2. Telling your friends, relatives, and associates how you're going to "beat the system".
3. Telling people you have a trust (and even where it is and what its called!). Investigators will lie, cheat, and steal to get at it. They will also threaten or bribe friends and relatives.

4. Making $100,000 one year and then claiming to make nothing or next to nothing the next (tax collector flag).
5. Building up debt while having assets, then declaring bankruptcy and claiming to have no assets (courts may say any asset transfer done two years prior to the bankruptcy was fraudulent and/or intended to avoid financial responsibilities).
6. Obviously living beyond your means - be discreet and always maintain a low profile.
7. Making many trips outside the country. More than four trips a year, especially to the Caribbean, is considered suspicious (you are obviously a drug dealer laundering money).
8. Renewing a professional license without considering the implications of sensitive information recorded on the license.
9. Calling toll-free numbers from a secure phone (these always reveal where the call originated.)
10. Being half in and half out of the system or co-mingling personal and trust funds.
11. Making many large cash transactions, especially with a local bank unless you are obviously in a cash business, like a theater or a restaurant.
12. Using cordless or cellular phones and revealing sensitive information of any kind regardless of whether its 900 mhz, digital, or analog (baby monitors included here).

If you think you're being stalked:

The main thing to remember is to break established patterns. Here is a list of things you can do to protect yourself:

At home:

1. Get an unpublished, unlisted phone and only give the number out to those you trust. All commercial or business calls will go to a non-secure phone attached to an answering machine (and is never answered) or to your work phone.

2. Consider purchasing a voice modifier for calls you don't initiate.
3. Alert all family or household members to be alert to unusual calls and to never give out the number for the unlisted number without checking with you first. If you have kids, maybe they could have their own unlisted numbers. They should still be very careful about whom they give out the number.
4. Assign all children pass codes for use under unusual circumstances or in emergencies.
5. Tape emergency numbers on phones. Make sure your kids know about using 911.
6. Establish a third party (relative or trusted friend) who can take calls from all family members to report their whereabouts in an emergency. Make sure all family members know this number. You might also give the number to a member of the local law enforcement agency.
7. Check out all threats with the local law enforcement agency.
8. If you decide to keep a gun in the house, be sure it is locked away from children and get training on how to use it.
9. Stop being so consistent. Take different routes home or to work.
10. Eat and socialize at different locations.
11. Be aware of your phone calls. Don't ever make important calls from a hotel room.
12. Don't take any calls from your secure phone unless you have caller ID and are sure of the caller.
13. Always be alert for any suspicious persons around you on foot or in a car.
14. Check the peephole before opening any doors. If you don't have one at home, get one installed.
15. Install adequate outside lighting at home. Check that it is working and high enough to discourage tampering with.
16. Get a burglar alarm installed at home and at work. You may also want to install a loud exterior alarm bell that can be activated at numerous locations inside.
17. Install and maintain smoke detectors in the house.

18. Maintain good all-purpose fire extinguishers at strategic locations, in the garage and in the basement.
19. Install locks on fence gates and keep shrubs trimmed to prevent hiding places.
20. Install dead bolt locks on all outside doors. Check the lock on your garage door. If you use an electric garage door opener, be sure to use one with the greatest security features possible.
21. Place locking devices on all windows. Keep all doors and windows locked.
22. Don't leave spare keys outside.
23. Lock your fuse box. Keep flashlights available nearby in case of an outage.
24. Keep flashlight and shoes near your bed.
25. If you have any household staff, be sure to get thorough background checks on them. Instruct them regularly with regard to security measures they must follow. You may also want to assign them pass codes. They should also be instructed to never discuss any family matters with anyone.
26. Do not disturb any unusual packages, boxes or devices left on your premises. Alert authorities.
27. Use timers for radio, TV, and lights to make your home seem lived in during your absence. Have mail and newspapers picked up too.
28. Get a big dog and train it professionally if necessary.
29. Prepare an evacuation plan and instruct all family members on its use. Make sure there are emergency window ladders, etc. for multi-story houses.
30. Accompany children to and from school or bus stops.
31. Require positive identification of all sales or repair persons before allowing entry into the house. Don't allow entry if the call is not scheduled in advance.
32. Review your situation with trusted neighbors and provide photos of suspects and vehicles if possible.
33. Inform trusted neighbors, business associates, relatives, friends of any trips, extended absences, etc. so they can keep an eye out for your family while you're gone (or notice if

you aren't back when scheduled). If you live in an apartment, this would include the manager, doorman, and/or valet.

34. Park in secured garages if possible. Never park in isolated or unlit areas where no one else is available for help if needed.

At work:

1. You should have a receptionist for all guests and deliveries. You may also want them to screen your calls and mail.
2. Don't accept any packages you didn't order.
3. Don't accept envelopes that seem bulky or have contents other than paper.
4. Alert other office staff to watch for suspicious people, activities, or packages.
5. Park in a secured, lighted, garage if possible. Do not have your name on any parking space.
6. Have a comprehensive security policy, with emergency procedures given to all old and new employees. Be sure keys are secure. Change locks if an employee does not return a key. Consider re-keying whenever an employee terminates for any reason.
7. If you have a security person, alert them of your situation and provide photos of suspects and vehicles.
8. Be alert to anyone following you to work, hanging around the building, or being where they shouldn't be.
9. Be alert to any suspicious vehicles cruising by or parked near work.

In general:

1. Don't park in lots where you have to leave your car unlocked or where you must give up your keys. Don't allow anything to be placed in the car or the trunk except in your presence.

2. Have a locking gas cap or inside latch. This also applies to the hood. You might consider an alarm for your car too, including a kill switch.
3. Check front and rear passenger compartments of your car before entering. Check all four sides. Lock the door immediately upon entering.
4. Always watch for vehicles that appear to be following you, especially vans.
5. Know your travel route, including the location of police and fire stations, shopping malls, and potential congested traffic areas.
6. Never stop to assist stranded motorists. Never pick up hitchhikers.

Bugging devices

Testing for bugs is something that takes some experience and equipment. I will list below some of possible bugs and locations of bugs that you should look for, but you'll need some testing equipment to do a complete job. Look in electronic or detective magazines for where to buy this. A professional is really the only one who can do this job right. Beware of anyone trying to sell you a device that will find all bugs. There is no such device. Counterintelligence is a sophisticated business that uses equipment which may cost many thousands of dollars.

1. Look for active RF transmitters, sound activated systems, series & parallel RF telephone bugs on phones and phone lines.
2. Check for carrier current bugs on electrical power lines and phone lines.
3. Test for Infrared transmissions leaving the target area.
4. Inspect telephones and lines for normal operation, and inspect phones for modifications which would convert them into room monitors.

5. Inspect phone jacks and all phone wiring for splices and bridged taps which would extend the phone line to a listening post. Inspection should include all telephone closets in the building. Inspect the phone system box attached to your house and look for additional wires. You should only have one for each phone in your home.
6. Conduct a detailed physical inspection of the target area, looking for concealed recorders, suspicious wiring in walls, hidden microphones and cameras etc. All space adjacent to the target area is to be searched including ceilings, access below floors, and other crawl spaces. All items should be searched as well; ceiling mounted lights, fans & vents; wall mounted pictures, switches, electric and cable outlets; bookcases and books; furniture, window drapes, carpet etc. Bugs and cameras can also be located in radios, TV's, toys, plants, fans, and built-in fixtures in the kitchen or bath.
7. One-way mirrors may be used to conceal video cameras. Look at them carefully for discoloration with the light on and off. Also check to see if you can look behind them.

There's a great deal of corporate spying going on and most is undetected, or unreported. Things like gifts of desk pen sets or junk mail containing bugs, dumpster diving, or even recovering spent fax machine cartridges go on every day. Even if you don't think you have any enemies, you do have competitors!

If you are a victim of identity theft

If you think someone else is using your identity and you wish to remain in the system, you will have to make some careful decisions. First of all, think about the value of your assets, your identity, and your credit. It may just be easier to report the theft and then cancel all financial institution accounts. You could then establish new accounts and even a new identity. This is not an easy thing to do however. Good credit takes years to establish and your Social Security Number is the all-important identifying entity that establishes you as a trustworthy person. It could take you a long time and reestablish your old good rating. If you want to stay in the system, continue to use regular credit cards and get loans, etc. here are some things you'll have to do:

1. Remember to keep copies and logs of everything you do during this process.
2. Contact your local police and sheriff's department. Be sure to keep copies of all correspondence and reports you file.
3. Contact the three major credit reporting agencies. Advise them of your situation and have your accounts "flagged". You'll also want to add a "victim's statement" to your records. The fraud departments of the big three credit bureaus are:

   Equifax Fraud Dept. (800) 525-6285
   Experian Fraud Dept. (formerly TRW)
   (800) 301-7195
   TransUnion Fraud Dept. (800) 680-7289

4. Contact an attorney to understand your rights and liabilities. You may be wrongfully accused of a crime and the attorney will need to know this too. You may also want to consider legal action if any financial institution does not help correct your records.
5. You may want to contact the Social Security Administration, Fraud Department to report the misuse of your number. They may also issue you a new number (I don't know why you'd want one, unless you are so enamored with the system, you can't see living without it). Call the Inspector General's Office at
   (800) 269-0271.
6. Contact all of your credit card providers (you do have a list don't you, if not, go to your statements or look in your checkbook for names). Call them immediately and then write them explaining your situation. Keep copies of all letters and send them registered mail. Close all old accounts

and open up new ones with new account numbers and new passwords or PIN numbers. Don't use old identifying names like your mother's maiden name on the new accounts.

7. Contact your bank(s) and change all checking, savings, money market, and other accounts, using all new passwords and PIN numbers. Get a new ATM card and new PIN number. Remember not to use your old identifying name (like your mother's maiden name).
8. Stop payment on all outstanding checks.
9. Contact the major check processing companies and report the problem:

    Chexsystems (800) 428-9623
    Equifax (800) 437-5120
    EqCheckRite (800) 766-2748
    National Processing Co. (800) 526-5380
    SCAN (800) 262-7771
    TeleCheck (800) 710-9898

10. Close all electronic banking, funds transfer, and brokerage accounts and open up with new accounts with new passwords. Remember accounts established on the Internet.
11. Change all auto-pay accounts to coincide with new bank or credit account numbers.
12. Contact your local and long distance phone companies to cancel all calling cards and establish new ones with new PIN numbers.
13. Contact your state driver's license bureau and check if someone has tried to use your name for a new driver's license. Ask for a "fraud alert" and complaint form. Ask for a new driver's license and number.
14. Contact the post office to find out if someone has filed a change of address form for your name. The postmaster can investigate and redirect your mail back to you. You could also get a new mail drop address and have all your new accounts go to that address.

15. Contact the U.S. Passport office and alert them to your situation.
16. Contact the U.S. Secret Service and explain your situation.

An identity theft victim by the name of Mari Frank has written a book called "From Victim to Victor". You can get it from her web site at: www.identitytheft.org.

Private investigator secrets

Here's what they do and how they think. Some people and assets are easy to find because they leave an obvious trail. Others are more difficult, but a good private investigator has many tools at his or her disposal. A private investigator once told me that friends, associates, and relatives are some of his best sources of information about a person. He included family members, business associates or fellow employees, neighbors, friends, accountants, stock brokers, lawyers, and bankers. These people, whom most people trust the most, are an investigator's best source of information about you! Keep that in mind when you spread the word about everything you do to everyone at the office. They also love reunion committees which are always very helpful. Their most important phrase is "Can you help me?" People will give out all kinds of information about others to complete strangers, over the phone! Some things on the list below are obvious, others more creative. I'll try to list the methods in order of probable use. We're assuming the search is for a current address and phone of a person, along with a list of their assets and locations.

1. Look in a phone book for the area of last known address.
2. Call directory assistance in the state of last known address (here's why you have an unlisted number and no number listed in your name).
3. Use Yahoo, Bigfoot, Dogpile, or other search engines on the Internet to find current address, phone, and email.
4. Use a national phone directory on CD-ROM.

5. Call a librarian in the city of last known address and ask them to do a lookup in the Coles or Polk crisscross directories.
6. Call voter registration in city or county of last known address.
7. Ask for a security trace of header information from the three major credit bureaus. This will show all known addresses. A more thorough trace can be ordered showing credit history and employment.
8. Call utility, electric, gas, water companies in city of last known address and pretend to be the subject - get confirmation of address or phone.
9. Call state driver's license bureau (or Department of Motor Vehicles) and ask for information by pretending to be the subject.
10. Call county clerk and ask for marriage license information (driver's license and passport info may be available here too).
11. Call state department of vital statistics for state of birth or last known state of residence.
12. Check The Atlas Report for neighbors of the subject at last known address.
13. Check with Lexus-Nexus for information on all professional organizations and associations the person might belong to.
14. Check with state licensing boards for professional certifications.
15. Check with social and sports associations the subject might currently belong to, asking for general information. Often the investigator will say they're looking for an old friend and the other party will give them all the information they want.
16. Check with departments of hunting and fishing to see if the subject has a license for one of these sports.
17. Call the county tax assessor asking for information about property ownership, sale, or purchase.
18. Check with Secretary of State if the subject may be the officer or owner of a business or corporation.

19. Check the UCC listing in the Secretary of State's office for any state the subject may have conducted business in to look for records of loans or credit transactions.
20. Check with Salvation Army for location of homeless people.
21. Check with Army, Navy, Air Force, Marine Corps, or Coast Guard for current records if the subject may be in the service.
22. Check county, district, and federal court records for civil litigation.
23. Check federal bankruptcy court in state of last residence.
24. Check with the FAA if the subject has a pilot's license.
25. Call the travel agent most likely to issue tickets for the person and claim to be a secretary needing information.
26. Check with the International Association of Travel Agents to do a travel trace, or use the Airline Reporting Corporation for this.
27. Check with the Medical Information Bureau for medical records and latest treatments or provider contacts.

If the above methods don't find the person or assets, they will continue the search using more creative ways:

1. Check newspaper and periodical databases for records of the subject being in an article.
2. Check the trash at the place of residence or employment where the subject might be (especially looking for notes or bills). Even matchbooks tossed out will show where the person has been. Scraps of paper may have names and addresses or phone numbers.
3. Check the trash at the homes of relatives or loved ones, friends, associates of the subject, especially around holidays like Mother's Day and Christmas.
4. Surveillance of possible hang-outs or places of employment.
5. Calling the number for the subject and trying to confirm that they are there, whether at work or home using a pretext of the phone repairman or other phone company representative.

6. Sweet talking a phone company representative into revealing the address of a subject or ask for confirmation of an address by claiming to be the subject (or claim to have to contact them for some emergency or to get them some reward or insurance money).
7. If the investigator has a phone number of the subject, but that number has been disconnected and not reassigned, an investigator may call the phone company and pretend that he is from a large company that wants that number but must have a signed release from the previous owner and therefore needs their address on file.
8. If the person's locale is known, but not the address or phone, an advertising ruse is sometimes used, whereby a help wanted ad is run for all professions the person may be in.
9. Sometimes in order to get a person to show up, because they are never home, a fake notice is sent to the last known address, saying that the person has won a big prize and just needs to come down to some office to sign the paperwork.
10. An apartment number can be determined by going to the complex with flowers or a big box and claiming to be a delivery man, but without the apartment number, the manager will always give it out.

Investigators have even been known to use associates or travel themselves to foreign countries and bribe local bank employees for information. When you're making $10.00 a day working at a bank and someone offers you $1000.00, you have a very compelling reason to get the information they are asking for.

There are many other pretexts, tricks, ruses, and scams investigators use to get information about someone. The list is endless. If you must stay completely hidden because of a stalking situation or you were a witness against the Mafia for instance, you will need to be careful and not use anything that has to do with your former identity. Be especially careful when contacting friends and relatives. Never use any identifying information that has any connection with your former identity.

This includes mother's maiden name, names of children or pets, any previous credit or bank cards, and even hunting or fishing licenses. You must not revisit old haunts or drive your old car. If you bowl, try golf. If you golf, try bowling. If you were a church member, don't go and visa versa. Determined stalkers or hit men will cover all the bases. You can set up new and anonymous email accounts to deter Internet stalkers. See anonymizer.com for help here. If you're not running from anything, but just want your privacy back, you can follow the guidelines listed below, but still be cautious and discreet in everything that has to do with your identity. I wish it wasn't necessary, but, welcome to the new millennium

V. Big Brother and the International Banking Cartel

Can we stop the train of control that's destroying our rights and putting our lives and freedoms in danger? Politicians are supposedly our *public servants*! For that matter, so are elected sheriffs, judges, school board members, and all our state/provincial and local representatives! There's a big effort to control everything from higher levels such as the federal or even the *international* level. Individual, local, state, and provincial rights are rapidly disappearing. Federal bureaucrats and legislators seem to think that they know what's better for you and your state or province than you do. Their most common weapon is taxation, whereby they take a dollar of your money and offer to return a small fraction of it (either to you or to your state coffers) if you will do their bidding. Economic control has turned out to be even better than wars and physical threats because people can be "taught" to regulate themselves. They can be easily regulated by what they are allowed to buy, where they can live and the jobs they can have.

It's easy to blame government bureaucrats for our problems, but one must keep in mind that higher forces are at work controlling governments. In reality, orders are passed down from the highest levels of the international banking cartel. These orders determine treaties, tariffs, laws, elections, regional centers of power, business regulations, and even entire economies. Huge organizations with control of the International Monetary Fund, the World Bank, the Federal Reserve and central banks around the world determine interest rates, capital requirements, stock markets, infrastructure projects, and taxation on a global scale. International treaties even have a direct effect on *local* laws, as trade agreements may determine whether a local practice interferes with "free trade" through labor or environmental rules.

In order for you to truly understand how the international banks and governments around the world lock people into regulations using contracts and the power of money, you must read a book by Edward Griffin called Creature from Jekyll Island. This book explains the origin of the Federal Reserve System in the United States. It will help you understand how the international banks actually cemented their power and control by *writing* the Federal Reserve Act, legislation that was supposed to *break* the control of the banking cartel. In an amazing act of deception over the American people, the banks were able to consolidate their power over the money supply and the entire economy. This cartel is still in control today. It is able to start and end wars, determine national policy of any nation on earth, and control elections at the highest level. If you want to understand why you are taxed and regulated as you are, you must understand how banks control and create money. They do this with full support of the law because they *dictate* the financial laws. They carve out their control over the world using hidden contracts, artificial entities, and the power of the dollar to make sure that everyone obeys.

Make no mistake about it, you have very little control over national policy, whether you vote or not. School board members and other local officials are usually easy to reach, even at home, depending on the size of your district, but state and provincial officials are usually very *difficult* to contact. Federal representatives are even harder and are basically beyond the reach of all except influential lobbyists or the very wealthy. The international banking cartel even gives orders to presidents and prime ministers, especially those in smaller countries, who are completely dependent on so-called "foreign aid" and loans from the IMF and World Bank. You may be able to influence your local elected official down the street in your small town, but only a small group of insiders have access to the real decision makers in the world.

While you may *feel* like a real person, with full rights and an independent will, to international financial brokers you are nothing but a number. The United Nations is rapidly implementing an enumeration-at-birth policy in all nations of the world. Using excuses like public education, universal health care, access to vaccinations, and funding of a myriad of other government programs, global regulators hope to reach their goal of total registration of all human beings on earth.

If the parents of a newborn baby apply for a social security or social insurance number for their baby, the parents actually sign over the labor of that baby to the government. The name of the baby is connected with the number in an actual commercial contract. The name is typically written in all capital letters and is called their "strawman" because it is actually an artificial corporate entity. The entity is called a "transmitting utility" as it can be called upon to produce energy in the form of labor. In western countries, this capitalized name is used in all official government documents. The real (natural) person is then given responsibility for the *artificial entity*. Driver's and marriage licenses are actually contracts between these artificial entities and the government. But since real people *use* these documents, they accept the responsibility for their strawman and end up suffering as a result.

For example, in the United States and Canada, there is a natural right to travel on all public thoroughfares, yet you can get a "ticket" for failing to have a "driver's license" in your possession while driving on the public roads. The reason is that you accept responsibility for the artificial entity by participating in government schemes and benefits. The government uses something called "assumpsit contract" to say that since you accept government benefits, use the postal service, use a Social Security or Social Insurance number, sign and file income tax documents, etc., you can be assumed to be taking responsibility for your strawman. So if you get stopped by a police officer and you give him a government issued license when he asks for one, you are agreeing that you *are* the person listed on the license in all capital letters.

Who are you really? Well, you are a natural person and an inhabitant of the state or province where you were born if you still live there. Your natural and real name is *not* what is listed on your driver's license in all capital letters, but should be spelled in upper and lower case letters. John Quincy Smith would correctly be spelled John-Quincy: Smith. Note the hyphen and colon. The hyphen denotes that John and Quincy are both nouns and one is not an adjective of the other. The colon denotes that Smith is a family or clan name, so you could say that John is John-Quincy of the Smith family. Leaving out the hyphen and the colon and spelling the name in all caps means that the referenced "person" is a *corporate entity* and not the *natural person*.

All law really comes down to contract law and you must be aware of the contracts you are engaged in so that you can protect yourself. Ignorance is not bliss in this case. You must know the source of the contracts, the agreements spelled out in the contracts, and the penalties for not living up to those agreements. You should also know however, that you can cancel a contract, and void one that is flawed in its origination, or one that was fraudulently drawn up.

To learn more about this and your true identity, you may wish to study what are called corporations sole. National leaders, the Pope, Cardinals, and Bishops in the Catholic church are corporations sole. This means that they have reclaimed their inherent rights as sovereign natural persons and cannot be treated as a fictitious, corporate entity. They have declared the rules under which they will contract with other entities. Governments too, are corporations sole and operate under a network of contracts and treaties between other corporations. If you have not declared the rules under which you exist, they will incorporate you into *their* domain and deal with you according to *their* rules as their creation and property. Keep in mind that the state can only tax, regulate, and own what it creates. States create franchises to which people become franchisees, i.e.

individual corporate units who must operate under the rules of the state.

There are steps you can take to claim your true identity and your sovereignty. These may be completely unknown to you and probably you had no idea that it was even necessary. You have probably grown up thinking you lived in a "free country" and you didn't have a need to claim any rights because you had them already. I'm sorry to tell you, but the government's attitude is that you have *no* rights except those it grants *to* you. This is mostly because it has tricked you into accepting their assignment of an identification *they gave* you. Now you can argue that there was no validity to the "contract" because you were not of legal age, or that there was no full disclosure, but the state merely says that you have assumed responsibility for your corporate identity, have not cancelled it, and must therefore obey any conditions of it.

Refer to organizations listed in the resources chapter for help with regard to your real identity and your contractual responsibilities to the state. PMI Enterprises can refer you to experts in the field who can educate you about corporations sole, true identification documents, and legal/lawful contracting between you and any other entity. Until you understand *who* you are, it's difficult to know your rights. Be warned however, you must *assert* your true identity, don't assume you are who you thought you were. An excellent place to start your education here is at www.detaxing.com. Check for the corporation sole link.

VI. The Incredible Power of Private Contracts

The following guidelines are meant to be just that. Please do your homework. I am attempting to help inform you and do not claim to be an attorney. There is a lot of controversy with regard to Constitutional issues these days, especially with regard to the so called "income tax". I encourage you to follow your conscience and to assert your constitutional rights, but while doing so, protect yourself, your family and your assets. Remember, you can't be sent to jail for being poor, but you can be for fraud. Gathering information is best done without revealing your name, which isn't necessary anyway at this point. Once you decide on a consultant, your initial contact must be in person, not on the phone or through email. Discuss your privacy concerns and try to cover all the bases, leaving no loopholes. A competent consultant should be able to do this with you and should be very up-to-date on privacy concerns and techniques. Any discussion of your financial structure, locations of financial entities, or movement of any money should be done via encrypted email or in person.

Trusts, foundations, corporations sole, i.e. private contracts, are essential as the backbone of your privacy strategy, allowing you to disappear while another entity gradually takes over your financial "identity". According to *Black's Law Dictionary*, a trust is defined as: "A right of property, real or personal, held by one party for the benefit of another. Any arrangement whereby property is transferred with intention that it be administered by trustee for another's benefit." In other words, if I agree to take care of your dog for the next month, we verbally, or in writing, agree to certain stipulations including where the dog will be housed, that I will provide food and water to the animal, and that I will in general watch out for it's safety. We have a simple agreement that may or may not involve the exchange of money, but assumes that one person is trusting their possessions with another.

There are many different types of entities. Trusts are one, of which there are many different types, including short-term, simple, complex, Clifford, living-will, revocable and irrevocable, common-law, foreign, and statutory, plus many others. People are making up new names and creating different kinds of trusts every day. The main thing to remember is that a trust is considered a living entity, a citizen if you will, of the country in which it is created. It obeys rules of the country it is created in and, because it is not an actual person, it does not die, even though someone connected to it may. Therefore, it lives on after anyone's death, providing protection for children and grandchildren indefinitely. A trust can have citizenship in any country one may desire, as long as that country allows its people to freely engage in contracts. If the trust is established in a foreign country, it then subjects itself to and obeys the tax laws of that country. While the trust exists in a foreign country, one may control it from anywhere, just as many large corporations have headquarters in different countries than their home office.

Trusts have been in existence for a long time, going back over 2000 years. They were used both in ancient Greece and Rome. Basically they are an agreement between parties, providing benefits to all concerned. We can divide them basically into two different types, statutory trusts and common law trusts. To fully understand the difference, we must look at the difference between statutory and common law.

Common law comprises the body of principles and rules of action relating to government and the security of persons and property which derive their authority solely from usage and customs, or from judgments and decrees of courts recognizing, affirming, and enforcing such usage and customs. Under common law, we may do whatever we are not forbidden to do. Originally, the common law was created to protect the rights of the people and their property against the abuses of the sovereign king. The common law in America, is based on principles of justice and reason.

Statutory law refers to law that is enacted and established by a legislative body. It is in the form of written regulations drafted and approved by federal, state, or local legislatures. Statutory law utilizes the Uniform Commercial Code, revised Codes of the states, and local ordinances derived from the Revised Codes of the states. In general, statutory law regulates things that government creates, including artificial corporate "persons", actual corporations, and it's own agencies which supposedly provide benefits for its citizens. Everything else comes under common law.

It is very important that one understand the law under which one operates. Any one of the many simple common law trusts are agreements between parties and have nothing to do with government regulations or benefits. Indeed they are even supported by the Constitution which says in Article 1, Section 10-3: "No State shall pass any Bill of Attainder, ex post facto Law, or Law impairing the obligation of contracts." Many court cases have supported the use and legality of these trusts: "The pure trust does not derive any power, benefit, or privilege from any statute." Crocker v. Malley, 264 U.S.144; Eliot v Freeman, 220 SW 178. "When real and personal property is conveyed into a pure trust, it amounts to a complete transfer of title.", Carpenter v White, 80 F2d 145. "Business trusts are not rendered illegal even if formed for the express purpose of reducing or avoiding taxation." Weeks v Sibley (DC), 269 F 155; Phillips v Blatchford, 137 Mass 510; and Hodgkiss v Northland Petroleum Consolidate 104 Mont 328, 67 F2d 811.

Statutory trusts

These are most often created by CPA's or attorneys and have stringent regulatory and tax requirements. Their main beneficiaries are probably the same people who write them. They provide only limited protection for property and involve a great deal of paperwork and tax liability. They are often referred to as "Revocable Living Trusts and are required to file 1041 forms every year with the IRS.

Contractual/simple/pure common law trusts

Contractual trusts are instituted by a private contract, setting out the rights and obligations of all parties. The Supreme Court in Hecht v Malley 265 U.S. 144 described common law trusts as follows: "These Trusts, whether pure trusts or partnerships, are unincorporated. They are not organized under any stature, they derive no power and benefit or privilege from any statue." These trusts, including "Pure Trust Organizations" and "Free Enterprise Trusts" are non-statutory entities and are based on common law. They are legal in all 50 states (except possibly Louisiana, which is the one state that does not found its legal system on the common law of England). A simple contractual trust created in one state can operate in every other state.

The IRS has willingly stated that pure trust organizations have no tax or reporting requirements and are not subject to probate or estate taxes. Exchanging property into a pure trust is not a taxable event. They do not operate under any government laws or regulations and have no accounting, withholding, or Social Security requirements. They do not require or have Social Security Numbers, EIN's, TIN's, or any other federal ID numbers and can operate in complete confidentiality. Financial institutions may however, require identification numbers if the trust resides in the United States and attempts to open up a bank or brokerage account, or if it purchases or sells real estate. Information about the assets, liabilities, and management of these trusts is completely confidential and not accessible to the government or to the public. The corpus (assets) of these trusts cannot be threatened, seized, liened, or levied because of any debt or obligation incurred by the Trustees or the Beneficiaries.

Trustees and Beneficiaries are also not liable for the debts of these trusts. They are also free from all inheritance and death taxes as well as the associated legal fees since they do not die as a result of the death of any associated member (including Trustees, officers, managers, Trustor, or Certificate Holders). The personal bankruptcy or divorce of a Trustor, Trustee, officer, manager, or Certificate Holder has no legal effect upon the Trust. A Trust Certificate acquired during a marriage may be the property of the marital estate depending on the governing laws of the state wherein the couple resides, but an exchange of assets into a Trust prior to marriage, prevents a spouse from any marital rights to the assets and is not part of any divorce settlement.

A pure contractual trust is set up under an irrevocable contractual agreement in the form of a trust arrangement. A Trust Creator or Trustor enters into a private contractual arrangement with a Trustee to hold real and personal property for the benefit of another. After the contractual arrangement is established, the Trustor then transfers property (assets) to the Trust or to the Trustee(s) in exchange for Trust Certificates. After this initial exchange, the Trustee is under no obligation to the Trustor. It is agreed by the parties that the Trust transaction is neither a gift nor a sale. The Trustees and their successors as the Board of Trustees, are empowered to act as Fiduciary on behalf of the Beneficiaries, and to hold ownership as the absolute owner of the trust property (assets), for the Trust. The Supreme Court has ruled that trustees act as such, and do so as though they are totally different entities, and not liable personally (296 U.S. 48). The Board of Trustees may consist of one to three Trustees or more, who may appoint or hire officers to manage the Trust. These may include treasurer/accountant, secretary, or general manager whose duties include accounting, checking account duties, and protecting the Beneficial Interest Holders of the Trust. These officers may be assigned exclusive rights to open and operate banking, brokerage, or other accounts on behalf of the Trust, but are forbidden under contract, to divulge any information regarding the trust, to anyone. The Trust Certificate Holders may also appoint a "Trust Protector", who may intervene in the affairs of the Trust and is able to terminate any or all of the Trustees if he believes the Trust or its assets are being endangered by their mismanagement. Otherwise the Trust Certificates do not give the holders any management authority.

The Trust is completely private and its affairs remain confidential. It does not need to be registered with any city, county, state, or federal agency. On the other hand, some activities of the Trust may require recording, such as the deed to property owned by the Trust (unless the property is held in allodial title or has a land patent). The Trust has the same Constitutionally guaranteed rights as a natural person, including the right to own, buy, or sell personal or real property, develop, build, manufacture, or conduct any lawful business enterprise. It is also guaranteed the Constitutional protections from unwarranted search and seizure, and refrainment from self-incrimination. Even though it is a legally binding contract, it does not need to be drawn up by an attorney. Major activities of the Trust are recorded in the Official Minutes and include such things as receipt of assets, appointment of officers and Board of Trustees. The Trust is necessarily irrevocable by the terms of the Declaration. This irrevocability is essential for providing asset protection and avoiding probate. The Trust may set up a term however, with provisions for renewal. This term is typically 25 years, but may be longer or shorter and it may also be extended or shortened by the Board of Trustees.

The structure and residence of a trust is very important. For example, if you set up a simple pure trust domiciled in the United States and placed all of your assets in it, you might find that all of the activities the trust engages in seem to be open to the perusal and examination of all the same financial institutions and government agencies that your personal business affairs are open to. Furthermore, creditors or the IRS may seem to be able to gain access to all of your records, seize or lien your assets, and claim that you owe taxes, interest, or penalties as a result of activities of your trust. Wait, you say, I thought I was protected from all of these things! You forgot some important points spelled out above! First of all, the trust exists as an entity in the country where it was created. It is subject to the laws of that country. But, you say, I thought that the Constitution protected my trust from intrusion and separated it from statutory regulation! Well yes, but now let's enter the real world. When agencies of the federal government like the IRS or Revenue Canada, or predatory creditors such as banks want your money, they will stop at nothing to get it. Always keep in mind that U.S. and Canadian banks will always cooperate fully with federal agencies regardless of the Constitution or the law. You may find that your trust has been penetrated on the flimsiest of excuses and your assets seized. It is then up to you to assert your rights and you may be without any money to assert them *with*! Would you be willing to walk into a lion's den holding a sign saying: "Lions are prohibited from attacking human beings." One of the things the IRS loves to do is to claim that assets were transferred into a trust fraudulently because they were transferred within two years of the time in question, therefore the person had planned to move them to avoid their responsibilities.

Another thing that happens is that a person gets into an accident with a vehicle that is owned by a trust or a business owned by a trust is involved in a lawsuit. If everything else they have is also owned by the same trust, the plaintiff goes after everything within the trust, regardless of its status or involvement in the dispute. Consequently, the person loses all or some of the other assets held by the trust when the judge renders it a sham entity and allows general plunder by the plaintiff to ensue. Remember, lawsuits are about money, and lawyers follow paper trails to wherever the money or assets are located.

For the reasons listed above, trusts need to be structured and created correctly. Therefore I do not recommend that you simply run out and buy the cheapest trust documents available on the Internet or in a book and attempt to draw them up yourself. You will end up with a set of documents that are worse than worthless because they will give you the false sense of security thinking you are protected when you really aren't. You can go out and buy these trusts for a few hundred dollars, but they will get you *into* trouble, rather than keeping you out of it. Refer to the resources section for organizations that handle trust structures. These people know the system and can structure your trust to keep you out of trouble, giving you *real* protection. Keep in mind the following points when structuring a trust in order to provide the best protection and privacy:

1. The trust (entity) must be legally valid under both the laws of the country where you live and the one it is created in.
2. The trust (entity) should be created outside the country where you live.
3. The trustee must not live in the country where you live.

In general, a multi-tiered trust is not difficult to manage and provides protection and flexibility:

Master Offshore Trust - may be capitalized by an offshore foreign organization, may function as lien holder for the trust network

Domestic Operating Trust - may be a limited partner or operate separately, opening bank or brokerage accounts, invest in free enterprise and/or passive investments, may operate a business

And/or

Foreign Operating Trust - may be a limited partner or operate separately, opening bank or brokerage accounts offshore, invest in free enterprise and/or passive investments, may operate a business

Holding Trust 1 - holds real estate

Holding Trust 2 - holds vehicle(s)

Holding Trust 3 - holds boat

.

.

.

Holding Trust x - holds valuables (art/jewelry, etc.)

The Master Offshore Trust can serve as a master holding trust for all the others existing beneath it. There are separate holding trusts for each significant piece of property, especially those that may be exposed to liabilities, such as vehicles that can be involved in accidents or businesses that could be sued. It is important to separate these entities so that exposure to one does not create exposure to another. It is also necessary for preventing a claimant from seizing assets unrelated to the event in question. One significant benefit is that the expense of establishing the trust is encountered once and large annual liability insurance payments can be avoided because the total estate is essentially judgment proof. If the operating trust conducting a business is located off-shore, the need for federal ID numbers is also avoided and therefore the link to the Creator of the trust, the Trustees, officers, and/or managers is broken. Ideally, you would become an independent contractor, hired by the trust to handle its affairs. All property ownership is removed from you, there are no taxable events attached to the exchange of the property, and you end up having NO assets. You are therefore a very unlikely target for lawsuits or spurious attacks by government agencies on fishing expeditions. You have privacy with flexibility. You can conduct most all normal business activities and financial transactions you formerly conducted, yet with confidence that these transactions will not be connected to you or accessible to strangers.

If you combine the above trust structure with a foreign VISA or MasterCard at a private bank in a foreign country there will be no connection between you and the money. In addition, the trust could engage in a business, purchase or sell real estate, or do anything else a normal person would do. Since no Social Security Number is attached to any transaction the trust is engaged in, there is also no trace back to you. Essentially, you own nothing and receive no profit from the activity of the business, but you can receive benefits from the arrangement. For example, you may want to rent a house that the trust owns. You may be required to drive a trust-owned vehicle. You may have medical insurance provided by the "company" (another name for the trust). The trust may also purchase airline tickets to send its employees on trips.

This all seems to be pretty straight forward, but you do need to follow some basic rules so as not to contaminate the various relationships that have been established. For example, you must be careful not to co-mingle funds between you and the trust. You for instance, would not transfer funds out of an account the trust operates to a local bank account in your name. You would be careful in how you transfer assets and would be aware of the "fraudulent conveyance" claim that the IRS and other creditors use to connect assets to you because they weren't done "at arm's length" or were conducted within the two year time period preceding the situation in question.

You need to be careful when dealing with banks in general, especially domestic banks or even foreign ones with branches in the U.S. or Canada. The feds have put pressure on foreign banks to disclose account details of their depositors if they have a branch within U.S. territory, since the threat to shut down that branch is too great to ignore. It has also come to my attention that domestic banks are closing down many pure trusts in their paranoia and even though they are only required to disclose records of "interest-bearing" accounts to the IRS, they may also disclose records of "non-interest-bearing" accounts as well. So if you are thinking of opening a local account, whether it be interest-bearing or not, the contents and records may not be safe. I think you would be well advised to consider completely private banks, and NOT have the account in your name. You don't need signatory authority if you don't write checks. You can use an ATM and then purchase money orders all over town. For larger purchases, your trust should do a wire transfer. Your name will not be on any part of the transaction.

Some private banks will allow you to fax instructions and then follow up with a confirmation phone call, where you give a secret account PIN number or phrase code. You could also work with an organization that sets up your structures and then takes encrypted orders from you, for further transmittal to a bank. Knowing the rules and right ways of conducting your affairs within a trust structure is important for keeping your freedom and privacy.

Working with knowledgeable, experienced people is a very important part of this whole strategy. Because the tax collecting agencies of the U.S. and Canada consider all money to be theirs, and because they often operate outside the law, you need to work with consultants who keep up with the latest structures and legal entities. You may want to back-up your strategy by including a corporation sole (a legal device for insuring the continuation of ownership). Trusts are often targeted for examination and you may want to use foundations or other structures instead. Regardless of the structures you use, they need to be written "in the truth" which means in correct legal and grammatical English that says exactly what it's supposed to say. This will often be the one component of whole strategy that makes you impervious to outside threats. Experts in the field of language written "in the truth" are Byrun Fox and Bruce Steller of Open-World-Network in Canada (604) 826-2347 or Sir Lawrence Leupol of the Canadian De-Tax Group (www.detaxing.com).

In any case, use someone who can set up everything without your name being anywhere to be found. You may have control or influence over what the entity does in terms of its business dealings or investing, but nowhere should a person be able to find your name as a trustee, grantor, settlor, creator, beneficiary, sole signatory, director, nominee, or owner (whether of the entity itself or of bearer shares). You should also not get any mail from the entity at your home address or an address attached to your name. It should come to a company address. You should not have a credit or debit card that that the entity owns be in your name, nor should your state issued ID, ssn, sin, ein, or tin be used to set up any of the accounts. Do not use a domestic clearing house to clear checks, but instead use a foreign facility. Do not use your home phone or fax to issue directives or letters of wishes. Use encrypted email instead. Do not use your state issued ID when using any credit or debit cards that belong to the entity. Do not sign any checks with your name for any offshore account.

All of these things will require that you set your entity (company) up with reputable and knowledgeable consultants. There are many out there and there are also sloppy ones just out for the money. Businesses are set up and managed all the time using such structures and you can do the same. Just don't assume that it's as easy as downloading some documents off the web and figuring it out for yourself. Once your structures are set up correctly, normal business processing and estate planning is fairly easy. Don't be overwhelmed, but do be diligent in your work. See the reference section for organizations that can help.

VII. References and Resources

Laws that affect your privacy rights

The Telephone Consumer Protection Act of 1991

This law establishes specific guidelines for telemarketers:

- They cannot call before 8:00 A.M. or after 9:00 P.M.
- They must place you on a "don't call" list if you request, and agree not to call you again or give your number to any others.
- It prohibits the use of artificial or prerecorded voice messages such as computer generated calls or questionnaires.
- Telemarketers must disclose to the consumer, the name of the individual caller's name, the name of the person or entity on whose behalf the call is being made, and the phone number or address at which the caller or entity can be reached.

The Freedom of Information Act

This law is helpful in obtaining copies of local, state, and federal government files that contain information on you. You can request to see governmental records, but you'll have to contact each agency separately because there is no central entity that keeps or even knows where all the information gathered on you is kept. Keep in mind that your request may be denied if the information contains any data pertaining to an ongoing investigation, the CIA, the NSA, the FBI, litigation of any kind, civil service exams, or any confidential government sources. Be sure to contact the agency first to see if it's the right place and to confirm their address and phone. You'll also want to know about any costs involved. Check with the public information office of the agency and ask if it will release the information without a written request.

If you do make a request, be sure to give all necessary pertinent details like dates, addresses, and titles. You'll also have to ask that field office records be checked too in addition to those at headquarters, since this isn't routinely done unless requested. Agencies do have some discretion about what is released, so ask, even if you think the material may not be released. If you are denied, you can request that the agency cite specific reasons for each item that is denied. This will help you in case you decide to appeal. This may take the form of an administrative appeal or one processed through the courts. You may also sue the agency to demand the information or to prevent it from being disclosed to others. In general, a request may be denied if it falls within nine exempted categories: information on litigation, internal agency memos, trade secrets, law enforcement activities, CIA related data, classified documents, "personnel, medical, or other files that would invade someone's personal privacy", and confidential government sources.

Request a waiver of search and copy fees, especially if you can claim that your use of the information will be in the public interest. It may be if it is for educational or scientific purposes, for proposing legislation, or for use in a news gathering effort (assuming you're a representative of a valid news organization). Indicate what you'll be willing to pay in case fees can't be waived.

In all cases, remember that your request is not a high priority item and because of a lack of manpower, there may be long delays. Even if you are successful, much of the information may be blocked out. You can even request that the FBI show you any records it has on you, but don't expect a quick response. You could wait two years or more to even find out if they have a file on you.

To read the full text of this law, see the following web site: www.usdoj.gov/oip/foia_rights.htm#TEXT
A good web site for this and the Privacy Act is:
www.oha.doe.gov/foiar.htm

You can also learn more, including how to request records, from the following web sites:
www.aclu.org/library/foia.html
www.tncrimlaw.com/foia_indx.html
www.usdoj.gov/oip/oip.html

To order *A Citizen's Guide to Using the Freedom of Information Act* and the *Privacy Act of 1974* (Report No. 103-104) write to:

U.S. Government Printing Office
Superintendent of Documents
Washington, D.C. 20402
(202) 512-1800
www.access.gpo.gov/su_docs

A sample letter appears below:

[Date]
[Agency Head or FOIA Officer]
[Name of Agency]
[Address]

To whom it may concern:

Under the Freedom of Information Act, 5 USC, subsection 552a, I am requesting access to, or copies of the following documents [identify the records you want here and be as specific as possible].

If there are any fees for copying or searching the records or information, please inform me of these fees before fulfilling my request. You may supply the records or information without informing me if the cost does not exceed [$_____] which I agree to pay.

I am requesting these documents [or these records] for the purposes of:
[information for personal, not commercial use]
[a news gathering effort on behalf of [name of organization] in the public interest and not for commercial use]
[for scholarly or scientific purposes as an affiliate of an educational or noncommercial scientific institution [name of organization] and not for commercial use]
[information for use in a private business]

[Optional] I request a waiver of all fees for this request. The information is in the public interest and is not intended for commercial purposes.

If you deny any or all of this request, please cite each specific exemption that justifies your denial. Please also notify me of the appeal procedures available to me under the law.

Sincerely,

Name
Address
City, State, Zip

A sample appeal letter follows:

[Date]
[Agency Head or Appeal Officer]
[Name of Agency]
[Address]

Re: Freedom of Information Act Appeal
Dear ___________:

This is an appeal under the Freedom of Information Act.

On [date], I requested documents under the Freedom of Information Act. My request was assigned the following identification number: ____________. I was denied access to these documents in a letter signed by [name of official]. I appeal the denial of my request.

[Optional] The documents denied must be disclosed under the FOIA because ______________.

[Optional] I appeal the denial of my request for a waiver of fees because ____________. (Same thing for requirements for payment of review costs or search charges).

Thank-you for your consideration of this appeal.

Sincerely,

Name
Address
City, State, Zip

The Charter of Rights and Freedoms in Canada

Though it isn't specifically enumerated in the Charter of Rights and Freedoms, the Supreme Court of Canada has tended to interpret privacy as a basic right.

The Fair Credit Reporting Act

This law of 1970 gave consumers the right to know what was in their credit files and to demand corrections, however, as of the date of this publication, no federal law protects the confidentiality of medical records. The so-called Patients Rights Act actually reduces your medical privacy protections.

The Privacy Act of 1974

Pub. L. 93-579, in section 7, which is the primary law affecting the use of Social Security Numbers, requires that any federal, state, or local government agency that requests your Social Security Number has to tell you four things:

1. The authority (whether granted by statute, or by executive order of the President) which authorizes the solicitation of the information and whether disclosure of such information is mandatory or voluntary
2. The principal purposes for which the information is intended to be used
3. The routine uses which may be made of the information, as published annually in the Federal Register
4. The effects on you, if any, of not providing all or any part of the requested information.

The Act requires state and local agencies which request the SSN to inform the individual of only three things:

1. Whether the disclosure is mandatory or voluntary,

2. By what statutory or other authority the SSN is solicited,
3. What uses will be made of the number.

This act can also be used to request information kept on you by governmental agencies. It's purpose was originally to help keep information about you confidential. It supposedly requires federal agencies to collect only "necessary" information and gives citizens the right to see, copy, and correct those files. In addition, it makes it illegal for Federal, state, and local government agencies to deny any rights, privileges or benefits to individuals who refuse to provide their Social Security Numbers unless the disclosure is required by Federal statute, or the disclosure is to an agency for use in a record system which required the SSN before 1975. (5 USC 552a note). So anytime you're dealing with a government institution and you're asked for your Social Security Number, look for a Privacy Act Statement. If there isn't one, complain and don't disclose your number. If the statement is present, read it. Once you've read the explanation of whether the number is optional or required, and what will be done with your number if you provide it, you'll be able to decide for yourself whether to fill in the number.

Intelligence or law enforcement agencies can exclude entire systems of records from the review of the person they concern. See the section above on The Freedom of Information Act for general guidelines. You should assume however, that any information kept on you, whether it is correct or not, is available to the CIA, FBI, NSA, and other governmental security agencies (and the IRS). These agencies will not tell you when they access your records, nor will they tell you what they do with the information. Under limited circumstances, even employers can access the information and you won't be informed. City, county, and state governmental agencies also have access to your records and each of these entities may have its own laws or rules about privacy. Governmental employees have been caught "perusing" private records and legislation is just now pending that would make it illegal for IRS employees to delve into private information without due cause or authority. It may be easier to just establish a new identity and not bother with the hassle of trying to find out what's in all of your files everywhere (laws are changing on alternate identities however - watch for new limitations being made on this). See the section on "The Plan for Freedom through Privacy" for details about how to do this.

This act, while supposedly written to protect citizen's rights, is full of loopholes for Big Brother to walk through. The biggest of these allows information to be freely exchanged between government departments if it is for "routine use". Today, just about anything that bureaucrats do can be deemed "routine use". This provision has also resulted in the mixing of otherwise ordinary records with those having national security applications so that the overall file no longer needs to be shared with the one it is about. Furthermore, many bureaucrats interpret the act as only covering paper records and then freely exchange computer records (of which there are infinitely more).

One provision of this act expressly prohibited federal and state governments from requiring that you provide a Social Security Number before receiving services or benefits. Naturally, congress later passed many exemptions to this requirement and later overturned this section altogether.

To read the full text of this law, see the following web site:

www.usdoj.gov/foia/privstat.htm

Sample letter under the Privacy Act:

[Date]
[Privacy Act Officer or Records Manager]
[Name of Agency]
[Address]

Re: Privacy Act Request for Access

Dear _________:

I am requesting a copy of any records [or specified records] maintained on my by your agency.

[Optional] I have had the following contacts with your agency: ____________________ [job applications, loans, correspondence, etc.]

This request is made also under the provisions of the Freedom of Information Act. I am willing to pay fees for this request up to a maximum of $_______. If any fees should exceed this amount, please advise me first before fulfilling my request.

[Optional] I am enclosing a notarized signature that verifies the authenticity of my signature.

Thank-you for your consideration of this request.

Sincerely,

Name
Address
City, State, Zip

See Freedom of Information Act for sample appeal letter.

If you want to correct your records under the Privacy Act you might use a letter similar to the following:

[Date]
[Privacy Act Officer or Records Manager]
[Name of Agency]
[Address]

Re: Privacy Act Request to Amend Records

Dear _________:

I am requesting that you amend my records kept by your agency. This request is made under the Privacy Act of 1974. I believe that the following information is incorrect:
[be specific in your description of the information or records you believe are incorrect, giving quotes, dates, etc.]

This information [records] is incorrect because:
[again be specific and note its irrelevancy, inaccuracy, etc.]

[Optional] I am enclosing copies of documents supporting by belief about the inaccuracies of your records. [You could list them here]

Please [change/delete/amend] your [records/information] to read as follows:

[Optional] Please add the following information that [explains/clarifies] my records:

Thank-you for your attention to this matter.
Sincerely,

Name
Address
City, State, Zip

The Bank Secrecy Act of 1970

The official name is the Financial Recordkeeping, Currency and Foreign Transactions Reporting Act. It is very mysterious that it became known as the Bank Secrecy Act because its effect is to increase bank secrecy, but not in the consumers' favor! It, in effect, secretly keeps tabs on the customer. It is a perfect example of government "newspeak" that George Orwell wrote about. In "newspeak", words mean what the government wants them to mean, rather than what they've always meant. A word can even mean the exact opposite of its time honored and original meaning. This act explicitly sets out to provide the U.S. government with easy access to every citizen's bank records. Specifically it:

- Created the Currency Transaction Report (CTR) or form 4789 which is required to be filed with the IRS by all banks and financial institutions for each deposit, withdrawal, or exchange of currency or other monetary instruments in excess of U.S.$10,000.00.
- Created customs form 4790, which must be filled out whenever $10,000 or more in cash, negotiable securities, or certain monetary instruments are carried across U.S. borders in either direction. The amount was originally $5000 but raised to $10,000.
- Requires that any American who either owns or controls a financial account outside of the U.S. must inform the IRS of its existence. If the total amount of funds owned or controlled offshore exceeds U.S.$10,000, form 90-22.1 is required, which forces one to provide explicit details as to the nature and locations of such accounts.

CTR's are recorded in the Currency and Banking Database (CBDB), maintained by the IRS, and accessed through the "Currency and Banking Retrieval System". CBDB contains roughly 50 million CTR's. Actually financial institutions must also file form 4789 for transactions under $10,000 if they are considered "suspicious" under the terms of an extensive federal government list. Banks also now maintain detailed records of almost every transaction. This includes copies of all deposit slips and copies of the front and back of all checks drawn for over U.S.$100.00. Most banks also routinely microfilm all of the checks you write. Banks are also required to keep permanent records of all loans issued for over U.S.$5000 except for loans on property. The banks also keep your Social Security Number on file and if you don't provide them with it within 45 days of opening an account, your name, address, and account number is put on a special list that is given to the Treasury Department. All financial institutions are required to comply with the terms of this law. Financial institutions are defined as the following:

- Securities brokers and dealers
- Investment companies
- Currency exchange houses
- Anyone who sells cashier's checks, traveler's checks or money orders
- Anyone who operates a credit card system
- All accountants and attorneys
- The U.S. Post Office
- All automobile, aircraft, and boat dealers, property
- dealers, and settlement agents
- Any other institution that the government determines either constitutes a financial institution or might provide "a high degree of usefulness in criminal, tax, or regulatory matters"

This act was first challenged in the case of California Bankers Association vs Schultz. The banks failed to agree with him that the records were his and not the bank's and that the act violated his Fifth Amendment rights protecting one from compulsory self-incrimination, or his Fourth Amendment rights, which prohibit unreasonable search and seizure. Justice William

O. Douglas dissented from the majority opinion, but the act was validated and is currently still in effect.

The Right to Financial Privacy Act of 1978

The original idea behind this act was to require that the government get a court order to obtain your bank or credit card records. Additionally, the government would have been forced to notify the person of the request and provide them with the opportunity to challenge the release of such records. The problem was that the provisions of this act were just too much for our "public servants" and they were quickly watered down, so that records could be released for any "law enforcement proceedings".

The Tax Equity and Financial Responsibility Act of 1982

During this time, the IRS began to rapidly expand its activities, even comparing a person's lifestyle with his reported income to check for possible tax evasion. This act was an attempt to gather information that could bolster their case. It required banks and brokerage firms to report most types of investor income, including interest, dividends, and gross proceeds from the sale, redemption, or exchange of stocks or bonds. If a person fails to give the institution their Social Security Number, the company must withhold 20% of any proceeds in advance. Even barter organizations were required to comply. Furthermore, anyone who pays an "unincorporated entity" more than U.S.$600.00 in a financial year must also share such information with the IRS. Probably the worst aspect of this act was its allowance of the IRS to gain access to anyone's records by simply issuing an "administrative summons". This can be a written or even verbal request from an IRS agent for your records. In spite of the conflict with the Fourth Amendment, courts have supported it.

The Deficit Reduction Act of 1984

This act took the Bank Secrecy Act one step further. Whereas before, only financial institutions were affected by reporting transactions over $10,000, now all businesses were made to comply. Form 8300 was invented, on which your Social Security Number, passport number, and other identifying information along with the details of the services received, are reported to the government. Merchants are even asked to report "suspicious transactions" as well as "related transactions" in an attempt to determine if the person is doing over $10,000 in total business over the course of a year. Merchants are therefore asked to form opinions on their customers based on whatever they feel is appropriate. Precious metal dealers, jewelers, and even attorneys are being warned by the IRS about the possibility of jail terms and large fines for non-compliance. They have even set up a large number of sting operations, trying to lure merchants into non-compliance, then using lots of publicity to scare the rest into submission.

The Money Laundering Control Act of 1986

Because the government found out in the mid 80's that many banks and other financial institutions were ignoring the many reporting requirements of the Bank Secrecy Act, they decided to strengthen the laws and proceed against several large banks, publicizing the convictions and fines that resulted (some of which were many millions of dollars). The Money Laundering Control Act was one of the most onerous acts ever passed. It, for the first time, made "money laundering" a federal crime, made engaging in any transaction involving the proceeds of any "specified unlawful activity" a federal crime, and also made illegal structuring transactions so as to avoid any federal reporting requirements. The fines and penalties involved are some of the harshest possible and become even worse if the government can link the charges with the Racketeer Influenced and Corrupt Organizations (RICO) Act., which permits the government to seize all monies "laundered" as well as all assets derived through these funds.

The actual legal definition of "money laundering" is found in Section 1956. It states that it is illegal to make any transaction with the proceeds of specified unlawful activity:

A. with the intent to promote that activity; or
B. knowing that the transaction is designed in whole or in part
   (i) to conceal or disguise the nature, the location, the source, the ownership, or the control of the proceeds of specified unlawful activity; or
   (ii) to avoid a transaction reporting requirement under state or federal law.

What is an "illegal activity"? Well, tax evasion is of course number one. Simply depositing or using money on which taxes have not been paid, can now be legally defined as money laundering. Opening up a foreign bank account and depositing money you don't report to the IRS can be deemed to be money laundering. Long prison terms and huge, well publicized fines are what the government seeks to get. Over 150 activities are now considered to come under the definition of "money laundering". Even doing business with someone who uses "dirty money" can land you in jail. For instance, if you sell something to someone and you have any possibility of knowing that the money is from illegal activities, you can be convicted of money laundering. Actually, the merchant need not even be aware that the activities of which the person is suspected of committing are criminal! According to Section 1957, the government need not prove "the defendant knew that the offense from which the criminally derived property was derived was a specified unlawful activity." Even though Section 1957 only applies to amounts over $10,000, related transactions over a 12 month period that exceed $10,000 are also subject to the law.

Another new crime brought into existence by the Laundering Control Act is called structuring. It has to do with making many smaller deposits over a period of time that would avoid the $10,000 limit, by being less than that amount. You could be accused of money laundering if you merely made many deposits of $2000 over the course of a year (or even $900 each month for a year!) The penalties are very severe, yet a 1991 Treasury Department analysis showed that over 75% of the assets seized as a result of the anti-structuring laws were originally the property of people not involved in any illegal activities. In other words, you too can be a victim of Big Brother's quest for your money.

The Anti-Drug Abuse Act of 1988

Even though The Bank Secrecy Act had required CTR's for all transactions over $10,000, this act now gave government authority to *lower* the amount for certain "target" banking areas, including Florida, Texas, and southern California. Customers there are now routinely asked to file CTR's "voluntarily" for cash transactions of as little as $100.00. Also, banks are now required to keep permanent records of cash sales for all monetary instruments for more than $3000.00. These instruments include bank checks, cashier's checks, traveler's checks, and money orders. In addition to the new reporting requirements, this law allowed the government to seize your assets if all or part of them came from a friend or relative suspected of a drug-related crime! Once the government gets your property, you have to prove that you knew nothing of the suspected criminal activity. Furthermore, even if the suspect is completely cleared of any wrongdoing, but if your reputation or life is ruined in the course of the whole affair, you have little recourse. As a matter of fact, the law specifically protects banks from prosecution if they release your records and allow the seizing of your funds, ruining your finances and reputation, even if the entire case eventually absolves you of any involvement in any crime.

The Annunzio-Wylie Anti-Money Laundering Act

Because the government wants to cover any possible way for anyone to avoid reporting all of their financial transactions of any importance, this act was passed to fill any loopholes. Its purpose is to make just about any attempt to avoid any reporting requirements fall under the definition of structuring. The important thing about this act though was that it put tremendous pressure on banks to do the record keeping. Most importantly, the government could take over any bank they accuse of money laundering and can also prohibit any bank manager accused of a money laundering offense from working in any financial institution, even if he is eventually acquitted of any wrongdoing. Because of this, bankers owe their allegiance first of all to the government, secondly to their stock holders, and only thirdly to you their customer. In other words, as far as your financial privacy is concerned, the government is your worst enemy and the banks are next.

Illegal Immigration and Drivers Privacy Protection Acts

Congress has repealed section 656(b) of the 1996 Illegal Immigration Reform and Immigrant Responsibility Act (IIRIRA), (a.k.a. the "national ID law) as part of their Year-2000 Transportation Appropriations Act. The now-defunct section of law prohibited federal agencies from accepting identification documents that did not incorporate certain fraud-prevention and other security features. It also stated that, in order for an "identification document" to be "accepted" by a federal agency the issuing agency must have obtained the applicant's Social Security Number at the time of issuance. The "national ID law", slated to go into effect on October 1, 2000 specifically referred to driver's licenses, which would be "national identification documents." But the most important aspect of the current law is really the "National Identification Database." Documents will be of minor importance once biometric identification becomes fully implemented. The "identification database" is the key to the national identification system and has now been made possible via the Driver's Privacy Protection Act of 1994 (DPPA) which requires states to send driver records to a federal driver registry (and upheld by the Supreme Court).

The Legal Employment Authentication Program (LEAP) Act of 1999 (not passed as of the current printing), will completely reinstate the federal ID system by implementing the Illegal Immigration Reform and Immigrant Responsibility Act of 1996 (PL 104-208) which instituted "pilot citizenship attestation and employment eligibility confirmation programs." These are already underway in some states. The federal national ID was never dead. It has never even been slowed down. To stop it would require the repeal of somewhere between 20 and 30 individual federal laws; the first of which would have to be the DPPA. As long as the DPPA is in place, states will be forced to supply driver records to a central federal database which will be the national identification database. Almost all of the states went ahead and adopted the Identification Document (ID) standards established under section 656(b) of the IIRIRA of 1996 out of fear that the law would be enforced and they would not be in compliance. To stop the national ID now would require states to somehow be forced to "de-standardize" their driver's license documents -- which is not going to happen. The identification document standardization law, section 656(b), was enacted in Congress in 1996, and slated to go into effect in 2000. States immediately began to bring their driver's licenses into compliance. By 1999, most states had already purchased new equipment and were producing standard identification documents. In the fall of 1999 the law was repealed. It had served its purpose -- compelled standardization. Components of the new licenses are digital photographs, the card holder's Social Security Number, and interestingly enough, the "Driver 'AKA' Social Security Number" for alternate SSNs used by the card holder. There are 57 multi-length data fields in all. There are also standards for micro-chip imbedded cards, biometrics (finger imaging), and machine-readable technologies.

Together with programs and laws requiring identification for employment, the stranglehold becomes complete. Section 404 of P.L. 104-208 established the "Employment Eligibility Confirmation" pilot program wherein there was established the "citizenship attestation" pilot program. Under this program participating employers in participating states must obtain approval from the Attorney General before hiring any new employee. The AG-designated federal agency must first confirm (with the SSA) that the applicant is a citizen or otherwise eligible to work in the U.S., and then issue approval before any employee can be hired. Section 401(b)(2)(A) states that, "the Attorney General may not provide for the operation of the citizen attestation pilot program in a State unless each driver's license or similar identification document contains a photograph of the individual involved has been determined by the Attorney General to have security features and is issued through application and issuance procedures which make such document sufficiently resistant to counterfeiting, tampering, and fraudulent use that it is a reliable means of identification for purposes of this section."

Laws and the control of money

The above laws, in spite of their Orwellian names, actually do more to take away your privacy rights than they do to protect them. For this reason, you need to take every precaution to protect yourself. Remember that banks and other financial institutions are under great pressure to report even suspicious activity. Transacting business under the U.S.$10,000.00 limit is not a guarantee that you won't be reported. The government wants to know about all of your business activity, whether it be legal or not and what it wants most is access to your money. Banks are required to record all transactions over $100.00 for use by government agencies sometime in the future if the need arises. The name of the game is power and money, and usually power is derived by control *of* money. Governments don't have to conquer by war in the modern age, they can conquer by controlling the money supply and citizens' access to it. If you think that doing business with any bank or financial institution with a branch in the United States, or under its regulations affords you any privacy, you are greatly mistaken. For that matter, the U.S. government has gone to great lengths to pressure not only the individual states to enact similar laws to those above, but has also pressured other governments to do so also. Treaties have been signed that effectively create the same controls in foreign countries that are listed in the above laws. Watch out especially for countries that have signed the MLAT agreement.

The MLAT Agreement was supposedly created to catch criminals and has been used for that. Usually countries used for trusts will require that a person be wanted for a crime and not for some financial reason before they will allow anyone from the U.S. or anywhere else to have access to any bank information. This is not always the case however, and it's always safer to do business offshore in countries that don't have any financial agreements with your home country. Just because a country has signed the MLAT, doesn't mean that you can't do business there. You just have to be careful about how you do business. Many Caribbean countries, the Isle of Mann, Samoa (NOT American Samoa), Austria, the Channel Islands, Macao, and Mauritius (among many others) offer excellent opportunities for privacy in your financial affairs.

State driver's license requirements

State	SSN Required	Finger-print	Machine Readable	Digital Photo
Alabama	Y	Defeated	Y	Y
Alaska	Requested			
Arizona	Requested		Y	Y
Arkansas			Y	Y
California	Y	Y	Y	Y
Colorado		Y	Y	Y
Conn.	Y		Y	Y
Delaware	Y		Y	Y
Florida	Y "if issued"		Y	Y
Georgia	Prohibited	Y	Y	Y
Hawaii	Y (ssn=dl#)	Y	Y	Y
Idaho	Y		Y	Y
Illinois	Y (rel. obj.)		Y	Y
Indiana			Y	Y
Iowa	Y		Y	Y
Kansas			Y	Y
Kentucky	Y			
Louisiana	Optional?		Y	Y
Maine	Y		Y	Y
Maryland	Not required		Y	Y
Mass.	Y		Y	Y
Michigan			Y	Y
Minnesota			Y	Y
Miss.	Y			Y
Missouri	Rel. obj.		Y	Rel. obj.
Montana			Y	Y
Nebraska	Y			
Nevada	Y		Y	

New Hamp.	Y		Y	Y
New Jersey	Y			Y
New Mexico	Y		Y	Y
New York	Y		Y	Y
N.Carolina	Y		Y	Y
N.Dakota	Y		Y	Y
Ohio	Y if issued		Y	Y
Oklahoma				
Oregon			Y	Y
Penn.	Y		Y	Y
Rhode Isl.	Y			Y
S.Carolina	Y		Y	Y
S.Dakota	Y		Y	Y
Tennessee	Y			Y
Texas	Y	Y	Y	Y
Utah	Y		Y	Y
Vermont			Y	Y
Virginia	Y if issued		Y	Y
Wash.State	Not req.	Defeated	Y	Def. twice
W.Virginia	Y	Y	Y	Y
Wisconsin	Voluntary		Y	Y
Wyoming			Y	Y

The information in the above table was derived from information collected from various sources. Since laws change frequently, be sure to check your local state for up-to-date requirements. An excellent web site on the National ID is Fight the Fingerprint at: www.networkusa.org/fingerprint.shtml.

States are under tremendous pressure to comply with Federal regulations for official documents and we are being forced to give up more and more personal information about ourselves just to engage in the constitutionally protected right to move about the country at will. But you can at least contact your state DMV to "opt-out" of allowing your vehicle records from being sold to direct marketers. You can also consider just not using a governmentally issued license. You might decide to use an international license or none at all. See the resources section for obtaining international driver's licenses. Be sure to know the laws if you decide to go this route. A good site to check is www.drivelegal.com.

Private vaults

Use due diligence before trusting any business. A list of private vaults can be found in Jack Luger's book *How to Use Mail Drops*, published by Loompanics Unlimited. See the books section for this publisher. An alternative is to merely hide your assets, like jewelry, art, coins, currency, and antiques or heirlooms. You can purchase a book on the best places to hide things from Loompanics Publishers. You can also buy a home safe and leave it out, but locked, or hide it in a wall or the floor. These are available for under $1000 and should be fireproof in addition to being secure. One advantage to a home safe is that it is under your physical control. You can move contents in and out at will and don't have to worry about some bureaucrat or bank official deciding what's best for you.

Private mail drops

You have a couple of choices here, all have advantages and disadvantages.

1. There is the U.S. Postal Service box. You will have to fill out a form 1583 that requires 2 forms of ID, but is cheap and usually readily available. You may or may not be able to get your mail during non-business hours.
2. You can use a private mail drop, preferably one in a shopping mall where you can get lost in the crowd, or one that is in a more isolated location where you can get a key to the door and check your mail anytime. These tend to be

more expensive, but maybe more available. You will also be required to sign a form 1583 that asks for 2 forms of ID. Acceptable forms of ID include "driver's license, military or other government ID, passport, alien registration card, and birth certificate. The postal service has instituted new regulations forcing users of private mail boxes to show proof of physical address. They then insert this data into their giant computers. If anyone comes in and asks for the information for a box that is being used as a business, the proprietor is supposed to provide it, effectively destroying any privacy one might gain from using the box. Whether you could give them an alternative ID with a foreign address as on an International Drivers Permit, would have to be tested. Most mail drops allow you to include a business name along with yours for delivery of mail. A list of private mail drops can be found in Jack Luger's book *How to Use Mail Drops*, published by Loompanics Unlimited. See the books section for this publisher. At this time we can recommend a company that sells office space which you don't have to physically occupy. You receive an actual address, not a PMB and therefore ID is not required. The company will send your mail via courier every 10 days to where ever you want it to go. Cost is about $600.00 per year. Contact World Travelers Association at (314) 771-6680 (www.worldta.com).

Secretarial services

Secretarial services can be very useful for those needing real anonymity. These usually don't require any form of ID, but it's helpful if you walk in wearing business clothes when you ask them to set up an account. You can have business cards and letterhead already printed to indicate that you are official and legitimate. You can ask them to collect mail for you, answer the phone, take orders, stuff envelopes, or do any secretarial services you require. They'll even forward your mail to another mail drop, putting it all in an envelope and addressing it to another name. They are often more expensive, but the price may well be worth it. A secretarial service is more likely to be private and discreet with your mail than a lot of private mail boxes businesses. They're easy to find, just look in the Yellow Pages and especially note ones that advertise services for entrepreneurs. Call them first and ask some pertinent questions to check on their services and privacy policies. If you use the battered wife or stalker victim story, they'll most likely be very sympathetic and helpful with regard to your privacy issues. If you merely need simple services though, you could just walk in and set up an account to have them hold or forward mail and take calls (in whatever name you establish for yourself).

Organizations

PMI Enterprises
(800) 234-2854
www.privacysupport.com
Support and resources in all areas of privacy, identification, structures, and the private market

Open-World-Network
PO Box 3046
Mission, B.C. V2V 4J3
Corporations Sole, legal contracts, lawfully and successfully detaxing from Revenue Canada
(604) 826-2347
bfox@istar.ca

The UnTaxman Advisory Service
#11 - 617 Belmont St.
New Westminster, B.C. V3M 6W6
(604) 649-7446
Canadian tax experts and advisors

ACLU/Task force on Civil Liberties in the Workplace
(609) 683-0313
National Headquarters
(212) 944-9800
www.aclu.org

Citizens for Choice in Health Care
1954 University Ave. W. Suite 8
St. Paul, MN 55104
612-646-8935 voice
612-646-0100 fax
www.cchc-mn.org

National Coalition for Patients Rights
National CPR
405 Waltham Street, Suite 218
Lexington, Massachusetts 02421-7934
888-44-PRIVACY (voice/fax)
ncpr@nationalcpr.org
www.nationalcpr.org

National Employee Rights Institute
(800) 469-6374
www.nerinet.org

Freedom Law School
(714) 838-2896
www.freedomlaw.org

Alliance Against Fraud in Telemarketing
(800) 876-70060

www.fraud.org/aaft/aaftinfo.htm
Tips and help from the National Consumers League

Electronic Privacy Information Center
(202) 544-9240 www.epic.org
Information about all aspects of electronic privacy.

Newsletters

PMI Enterprises
(800) 234-2854
www.privacysupport.com
Monthly newsletter with updates on legislation, strategies, tips, Big Brother, and the information industry. Cost $35.00/year via email, $45.00 postal mail in US

Privacy Journal
P.O. Box 28577
Providence, RI 02908
(401) 274-7861
Monthly newsletter covering legislation, technology, and trends. Cost $118.00 per year.

Privacy Newsletter
P.O. Box 8206
Philadelphia, PA 19101
(215) 533-7373
Monthly newsletter Cost $99.00/year.

Privacy Times
P.O. Box 21501
Washington, D.C. 20009
(202) 829-3660

International Living Association
(800) 926-6575
Information and contacts for living/traveling abroad.

Access Reports
1624 Dogwood Lane
Lynchburg, VA 24503
(804) 384-5334
Newsletter covering open government laws, published twice a month, $325/yr.

Citizen's Guide on Using the Freedom of Information Act and the Privacy Act of 1974
U.S. Government Printing Office
Superintendent of Documents
Washington, D.C. 20402
www.access.gpo.gov/su_docs

Web sites

All of the sites below have information about privacy or other pertinent topics, but we cannot vouch for everything you might find there and remember web sites change frequently, so if you find a bad address please let us know. Precede "www" with http://

Privacy and security

www.privacysupport.com
PMI Enterprises - privacy services and resources
www.privacytimes.com/
Privacy Times electronic newsletter

www.privacyinc.com/
Privacy Inc. offers many services
www.ewss.com/
Expat Special World Services
www.epic.org/
Electronic Privacy Information Center
www.amug.org/~dbugman/elcnmes
Technical security consultants
www.teleport.com/~infobahn/spies3.html
Information about government and law enforcement intrusions on privacy
www.stack.nl/~galactus/remailers/index.html
General information on Internet privacy
www.epic.org/privacy/consumer/states.html
Lists privacy related issues covered by law, by state
www.ftc.gov/privacy
FTC site on privacy, includes how to opt out of mailing lists
www.cpsr.org/cpsr/privacy/ssn/ssn.faq.html
Information about Social Security Numbers and how to use or not use them
www.policy.com
Review of online privacy issues
www.privacy.com
www.well.com/user/abacard
Andre Bacard, expert on privacy and computer security
www.cdt.org
Center for Democracy and Technology
www.uwm.edu/org/comp
Privacy Computer Privacy Digest - forum for discussion of the effect of technology on privacy
www.cpsr.org/program/privacy/privacy.html
Computer Professionals for Social Responsibility
http://world.std.com/~franl/crypto.html
Cryptography, PGP and privacy
www.essential.org/cpt/cpt.html
Ralph Nader's Consumer Project on Technology

www.nationalcpr.org
National Coalition for Patient's Rights

Mail and phone marketing

www.mcs.com/~jcr/junkemail.html
Campaign to stop junk email

www.consumer.net
Consumer privacy and protection against telemarketing, junk email

Government

http://thomas.loc.gov/home/thomas.html
Look up information about any bill in Congress, including its text, status, and sponsors

www.findlaw.com
Allows lookup of text of federal and some state laws

News

http://cgi.pathfinder.com/netly
News site that includes many privacy issues

www.worldnetdaily.com
News you won't find in the mainstream media

www.hbroadcast.com
"Newspaper on the Air" internet-radio talk show on privacy, economy, banking, constitution, freedom, health, farming, how the government works, freedom of speech

Income taxes

www.ottoskinner.com/
Otto Skinner's site arguing that the income of most Americans is not a taxable event because there is

nothing in the tax code that imposes a tax on the normal selling of one's labor.

www.anti-irs.com

Bill Conklin's site entitled Why No One is Required to File Tax Returns ... and what you can do about it. Takes the position that filing income tax returns is a violation of our Constitutional 5th amendment protection from self-incrimination.

http://taxgate.com

Specializes in law references, and solutions regarding income, employment, and taxes for U.S. Citizens and businesses

www.untaxman.com

The UnTaxman Advisory Service in Canada. Seminars to show Canadians how to regain their rights, submit constructive notice to the government and legally deal with Revenue Canada from a position of strength and knowledge.

Medical Issues

www.conquesthealth.com

Medical preparation, (including Y2K) with privacy and individual responsibility

www.tetrahedron.org

Information about health care in general, supplements and vitamins, vaccines, and the medical establishment

Books

Stanley and Danko, *The Millionaire Next Door*, Longstreet Press, 1996. Living discreetly with a million dollar net worth - how *real* millionaires live.

Boston T. Party, *Bulletproof Privacy*, Javelin Press, 1997. How to live hidden, happy, and free.

G. Edward Griffin, Highly recommended! *The Creature from Jekyll Island - A Second Look at the Federal Reserve* about the creation and nature of money, and who really controls it. Discusses the real reason for "income taxes" and how your transactions are recorded to provide big banks and government agencies with the power to control the economy. American Media, P.O. Box 4646, Westlake Village, CA 91359 (800) 595-6596

Reg Whitaker, *The End of Privacy* Examines the causes and implications of today's surveillance 1999

Beth Givens, *The Privacy Rights Handbook* Well written with many references and helpful advice. Avon Books, 1997

Andre Bacard, *The Computer Privacy Handbook: A Practical Guide to E-mail, Encryption, Data Protection, and PGP* Privacy Software Peachpit Press, 1995

John Q. Newman, *The Heavy Duty New Identity* Methods of dropping out and changing identities (for whatever reason). Loompanics Unlimited, P.O. Box 1197, Port Townsend, WA 98368 (360) 385-2230. Order a catalog for other good books on identity.

Carolole Lane, *Naked in Cyberspace* Online, Inc., 1997, comprehensive guide to online privacy

Otto Skinner, *The Biggest "Tax Loophole" of All* provides the clearest and best explanation of the so-called "income" tax and the Sixteenth Amendment available to Americans today. Order this and other tax oriented books directly from:

Otto Skinner
P.O. Box 6609
San Pedro, CA 90734